COLLECTORS' SERIES

MASTERS OF THE DARK ART

VOL. 1: DONALD ENGLAND

ASYLUM
PUBLICATIONS, INC.

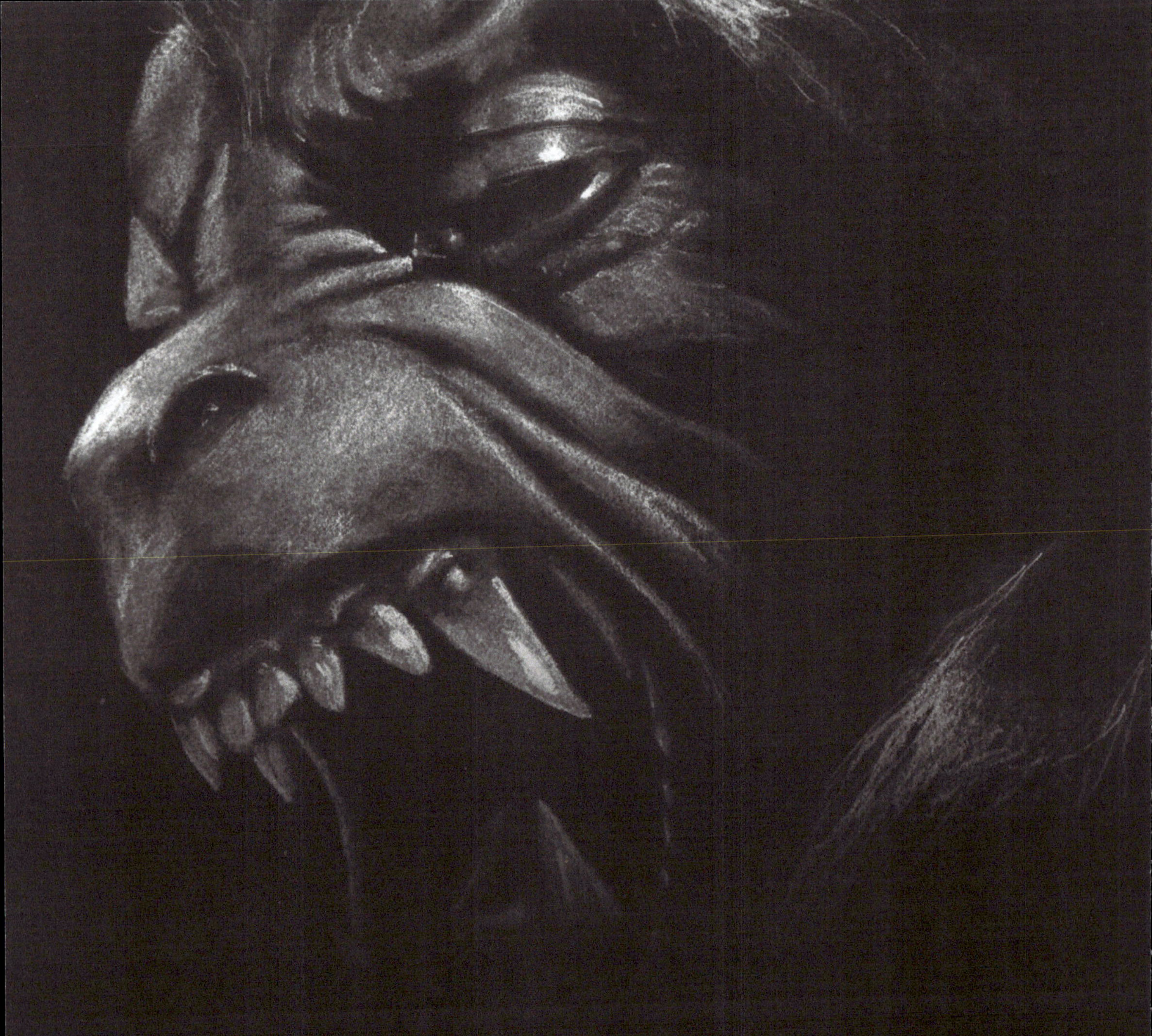

ARTWORK BY DONALD ENGLAND
EDITED BY JOSHUA WERNER & PAUL BURKE

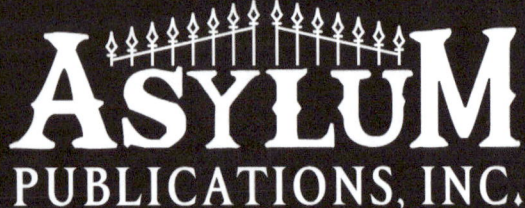

Distributed by Binary Publications

CEO AND EDITOR IN CHIEF PAUL BURKE
CREATIVE DIRECTOR JOSHUA WERNER

ISBN: 978-1-7339309-4-9
Masters of the Dark Art Vol. 1: Donald England™. Published by Asylum Publications, Inc.™ All images are © by Donald England. Asylum Pulications, Inc.™ and Masters of the Dark Art™ areTM 2019. All rights reserved. No portion of this publication may be reproduced or transmitted, in any form by any means, without written consent from the Publisher, except for any small excerpts for the purpose of review. For further information regarding custom photo/art books, ordering wholesale, or other inquiries, please write to asylumpublications75@gmail.com.

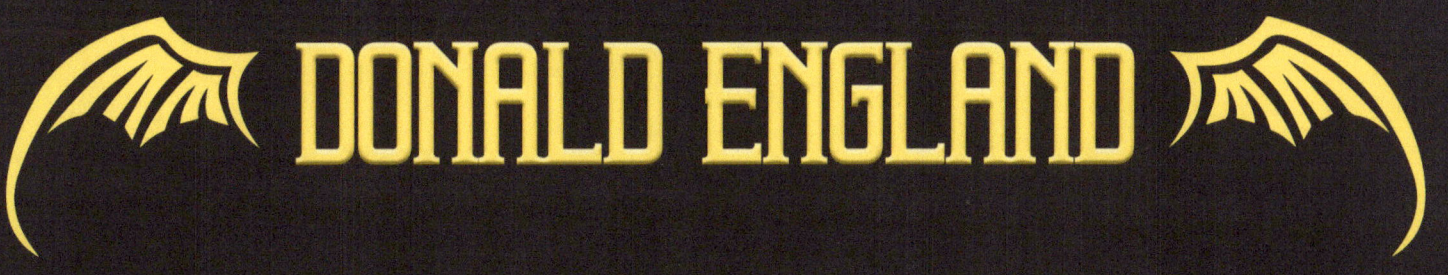

DONALD ENGLAND

Donald England is a Michigan based artist specializing in creepy and macabre art for the last 25 years. He is a product of late-night eighties television, comic book shops, and classic rock music. Donald is a life-long collector of comic books and movie posters from which he draws his inspiration. In the nineties, he co-created the comic *Lethal Lita* with Michael Leblanc, and worked on other comics like *Tales from the Ravaged Lands*. By the end of the nineties, he was primarily working on horror projects, creating catalog cover art for VHS sellers like *Video Wasteland* and *Video Dungeon*. Over the years, his work has been seen in a number of magazines like *Horror Hound* and *Liquid Cheese*, as well as cover art for *Evilspeak*. His art has been featured in *Late Night Snack*, *The Thing* and *Stranger Things* art books, *Deadworld*, *Cromwell Green*, and on the covers of *Erie Tales*, *A Fist full of Dead Folk*, and *Night Pieces*. He's also completed t-shirt designs for *Pallbearer Press* and *Rotten Cotton*.

For more info, visit http://www.donaldengland.com/ or find him on Facebook and Instagram.

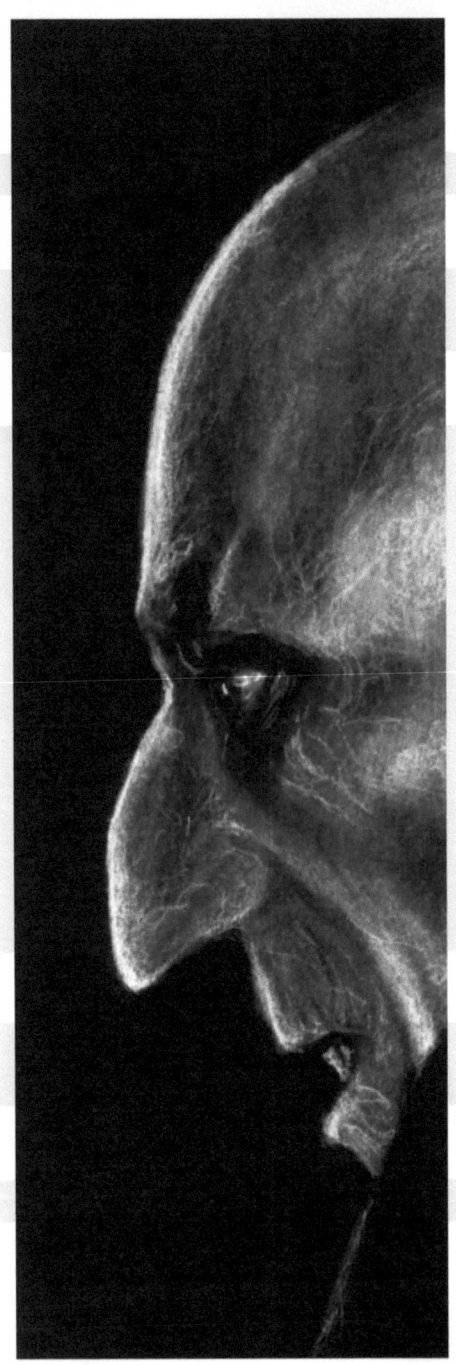
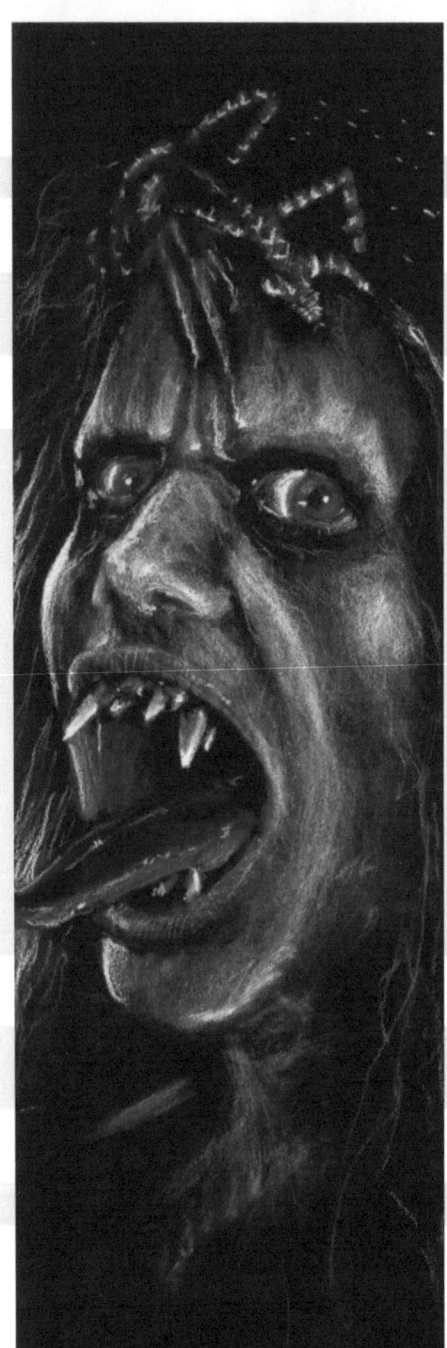
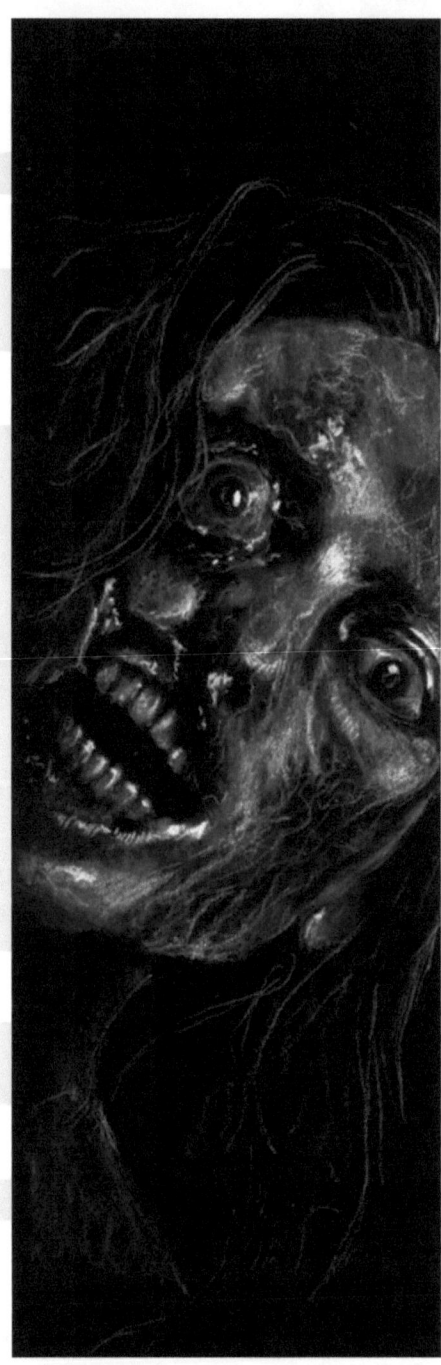
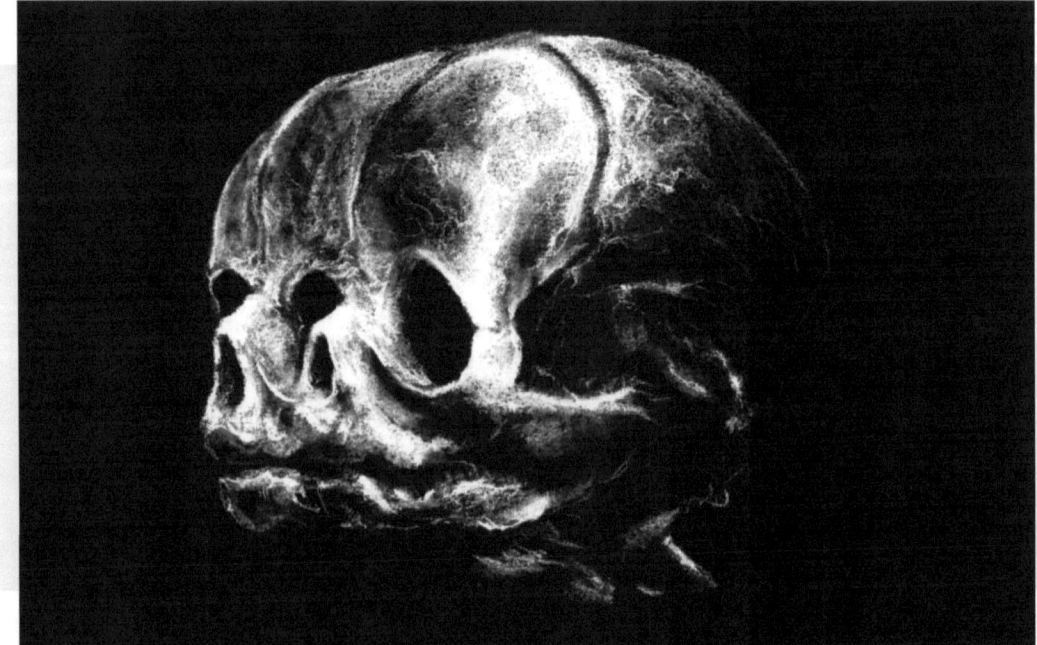

NOSFERATU
NIGHT OF THE DEMONS
GHOST STORY
CONJOINED FETAL SKULL
WHITE CHARCOAL ON BLACK BOARD

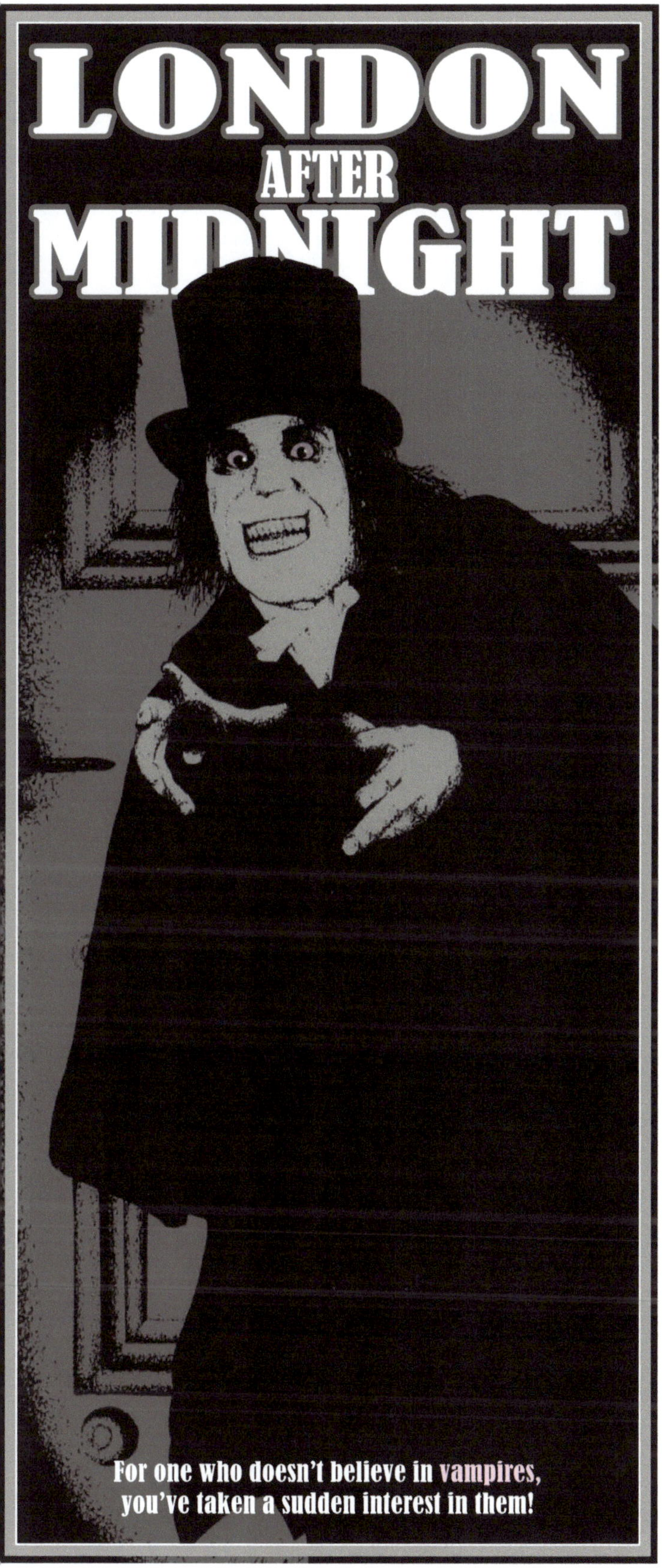

LONDON AFTER MIDNIGHT

For one who doesn't believe in vampires, you've taken a sudden interest in them!

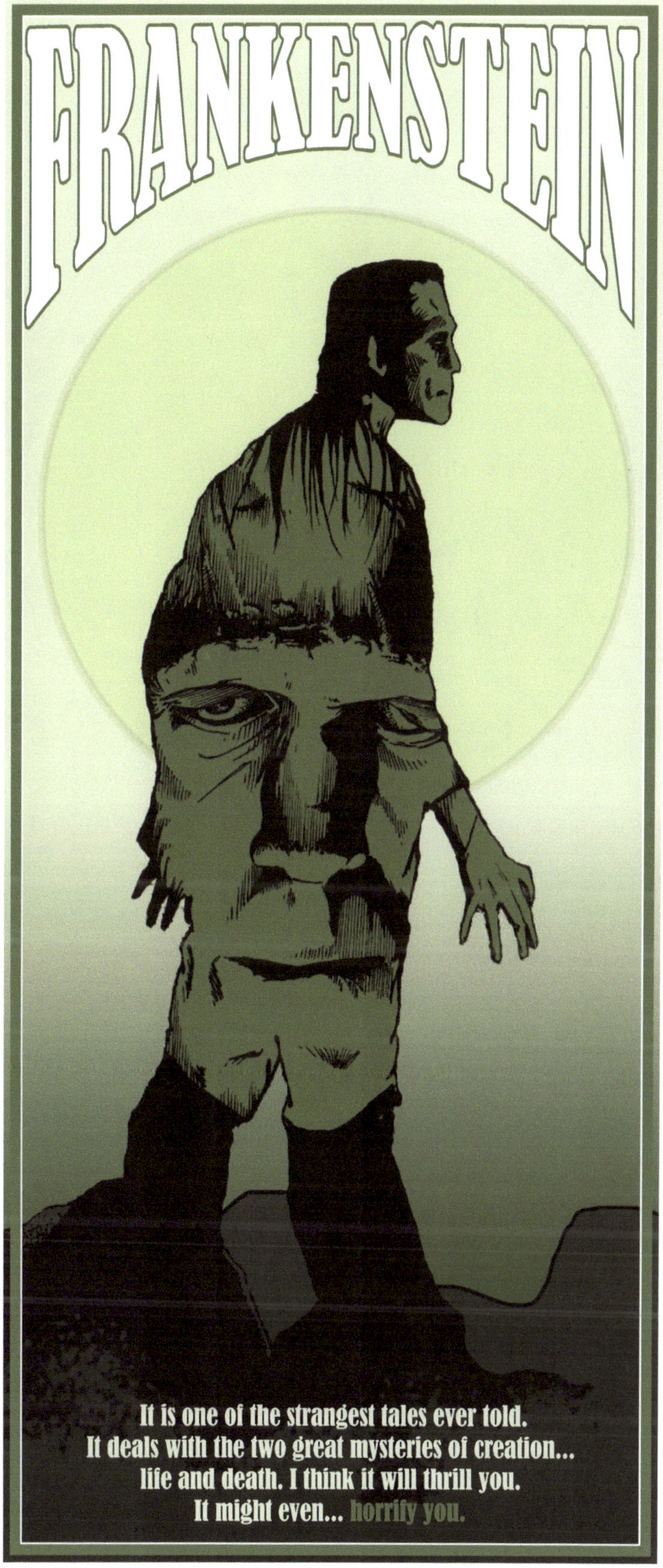

FRANKENSTEIN

It is one of the strangest tales ever told.
It deals with the two great mysteries of creation...
life and death. I think it will thrill you.
It might even... horrify you.

CLASSIC MOVIE POSTER DESIGNS
MIXED MEDIA

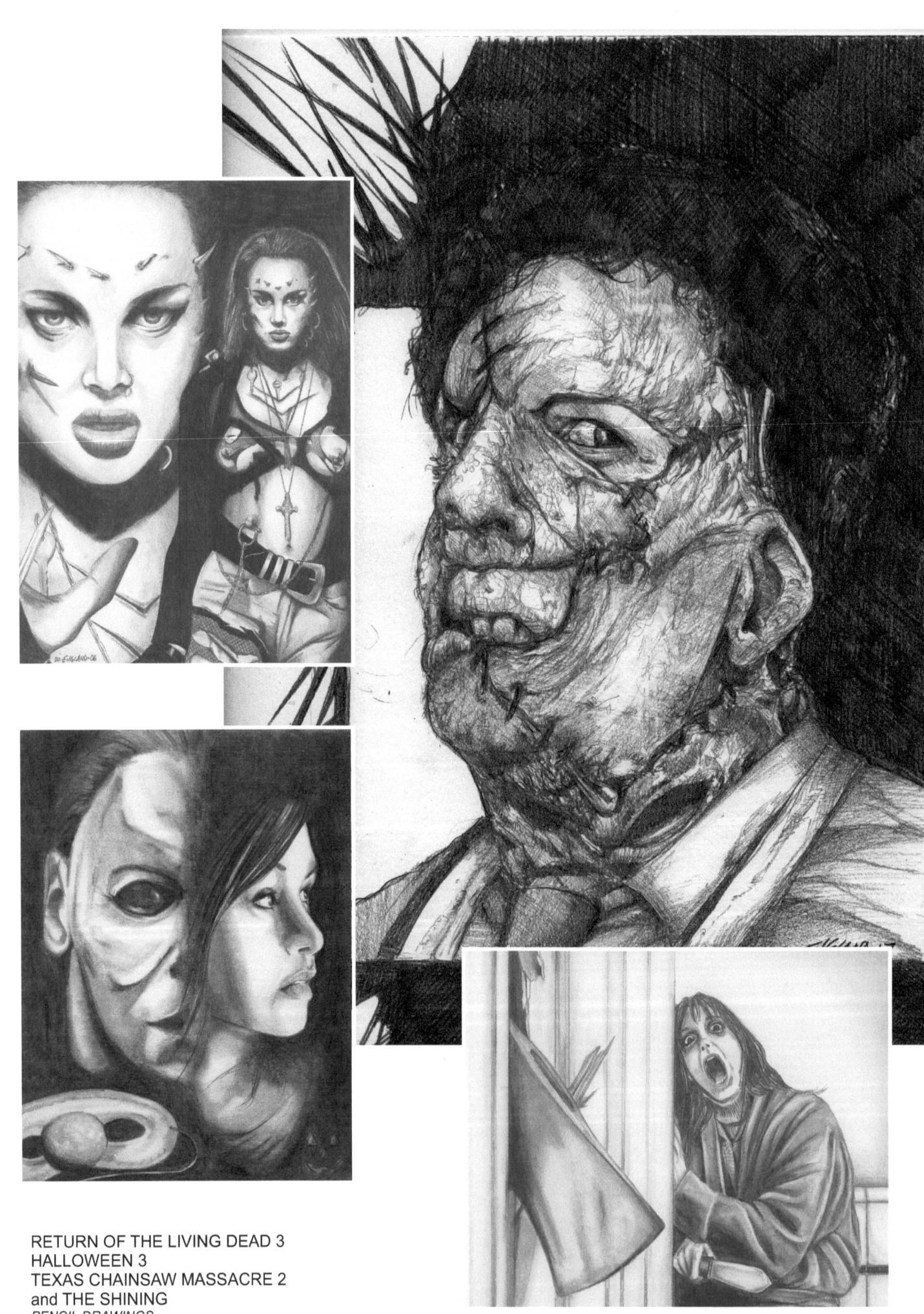

RETURN OF THE LIVING DEAD 3
HALLOWEEN 3
TEXAS CHAINSAW MASSACRE 2
and THE SHINING
PENCIL DRAWINGS

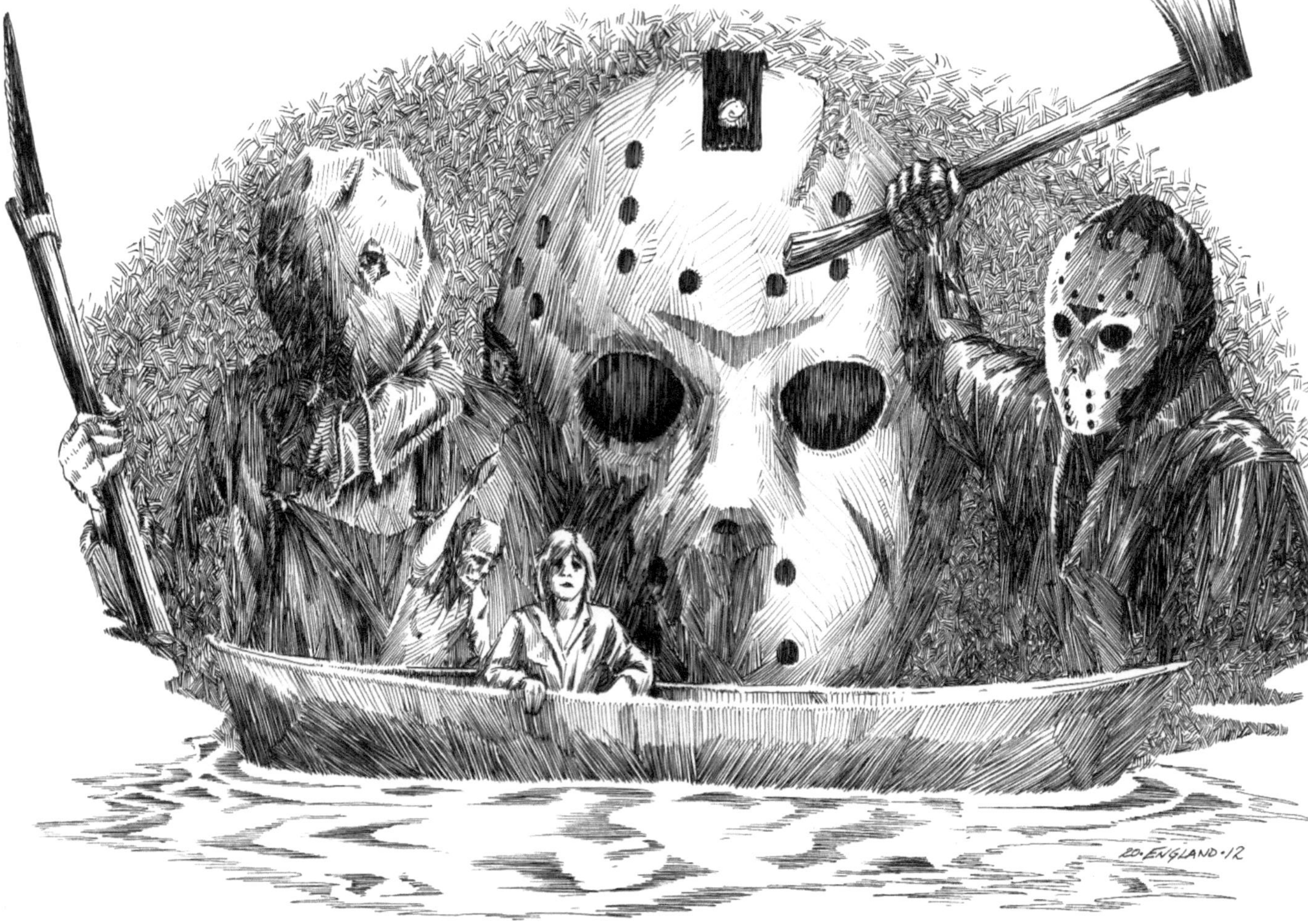

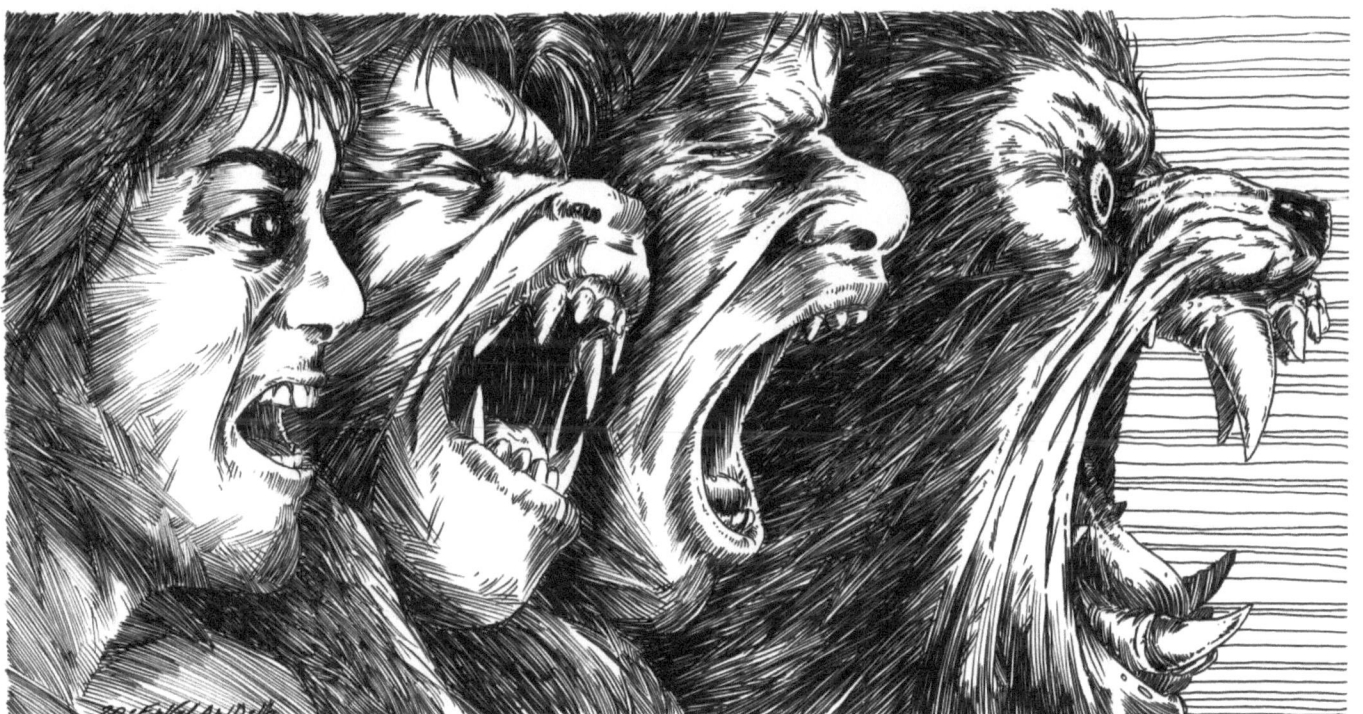

FRIDAY THE 13TH
PEN AND INK

AN AMERICAN WEREWOLF IN LONDON
PEN AND INK

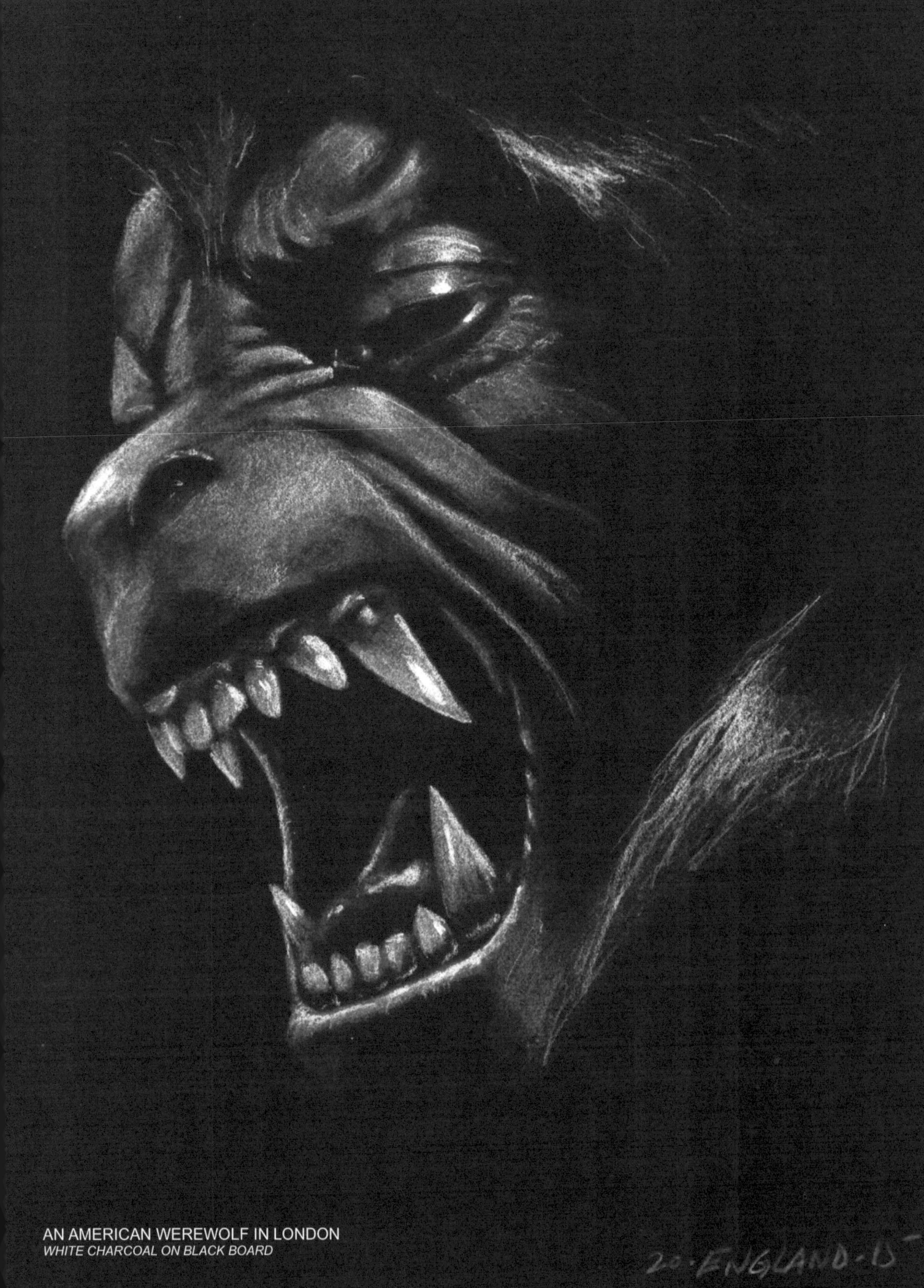

AN AMERICAN WEREWOLF IN LONDON
WHITE CHARCOAL ON BLACK BOARD

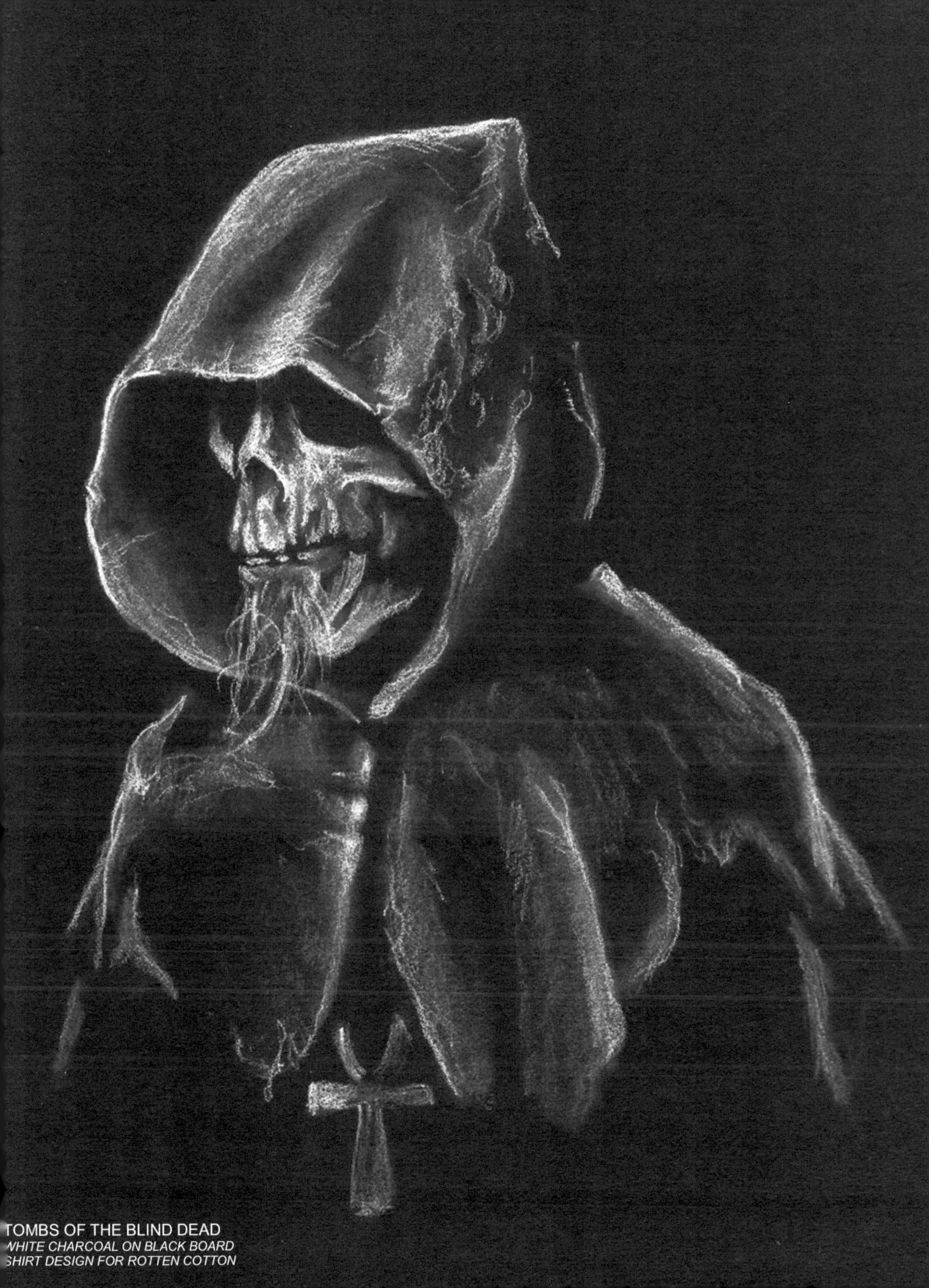

TOMBS OF THE BLIND DEAD
WHITE CHARCOAL ON BLACK BOARD
SHIRT DESIGN FOR ROTTEN COTTON

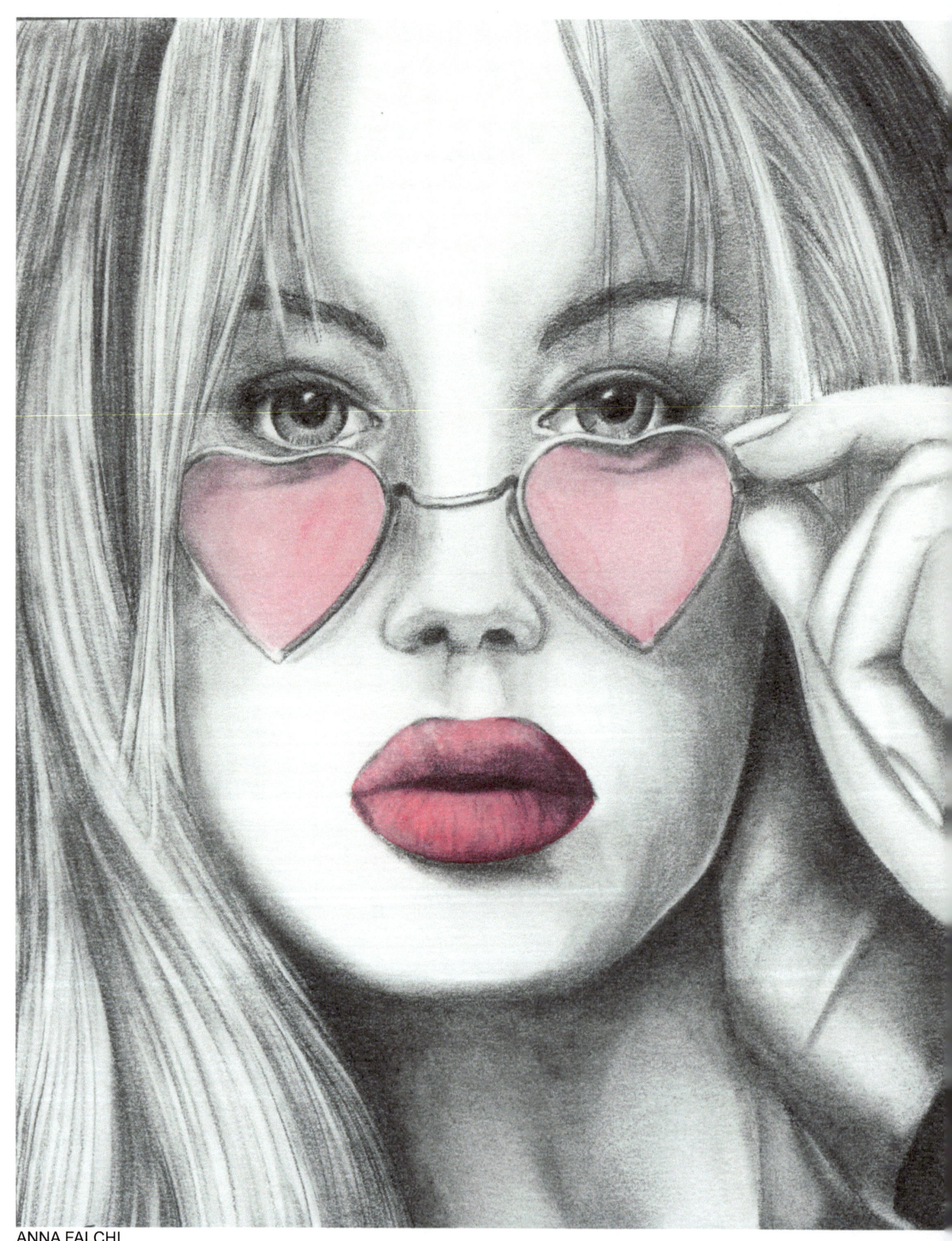

ANNA FALCHI
PENCIL AND WATER COLOR

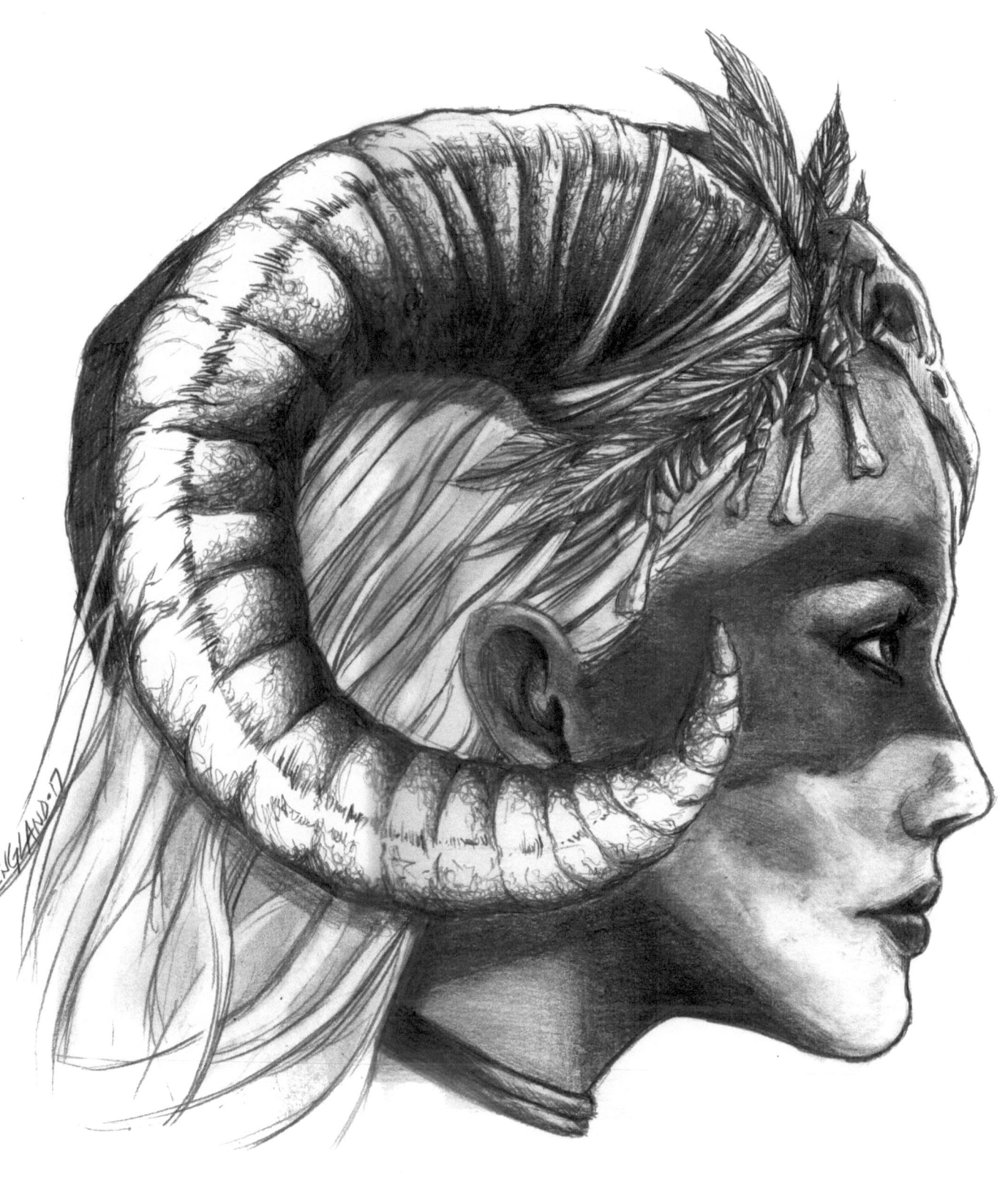

CANNIBAL GODDESS
PENCIL DRAWING

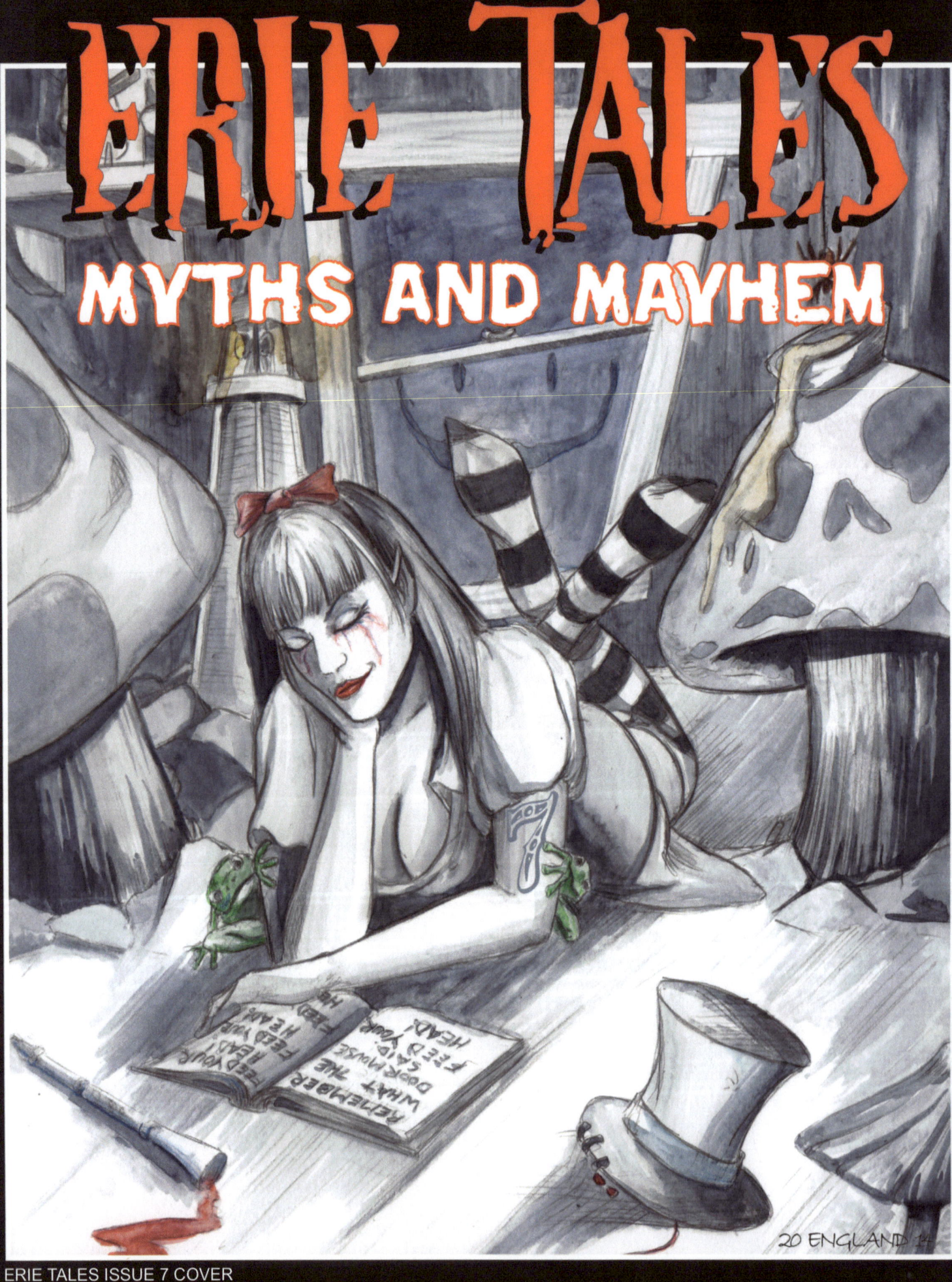

ERIE TALES ISSUE 7 COVER
MIXED MEDIA

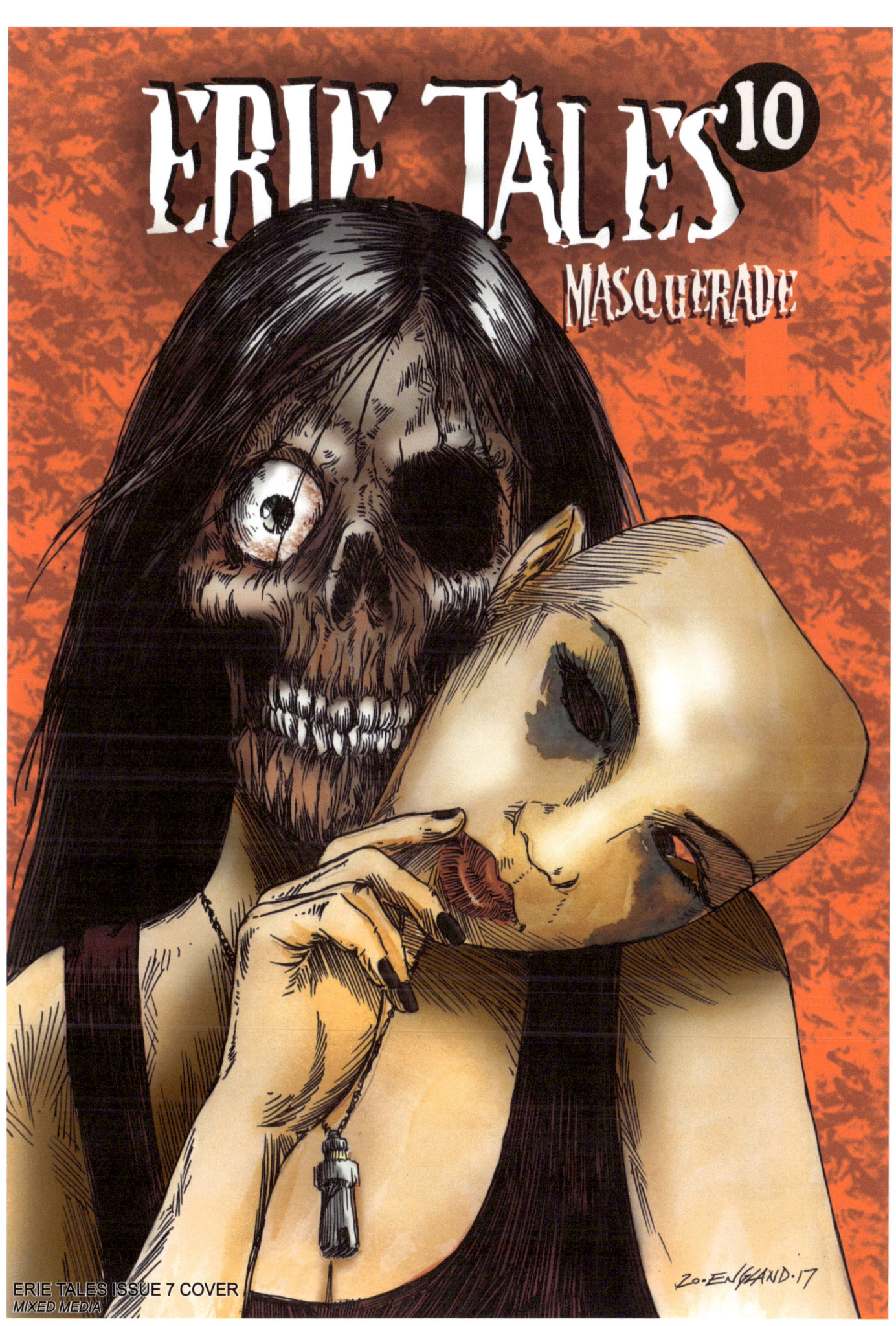

ERIE TALES ISSUE 7 COVER
MIXED MEDIA

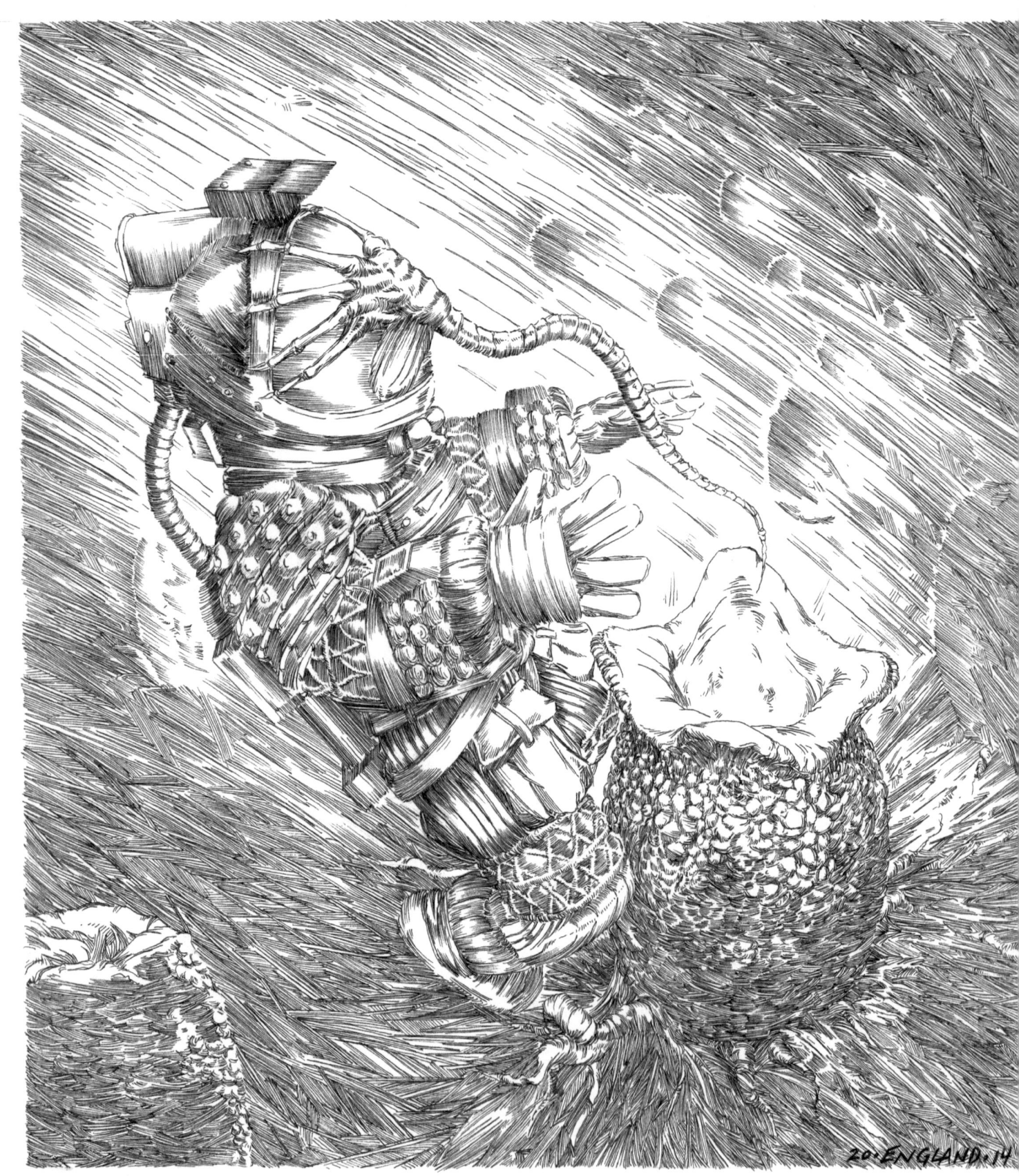

FACEHUGGER ATTACK
PEN AND INK

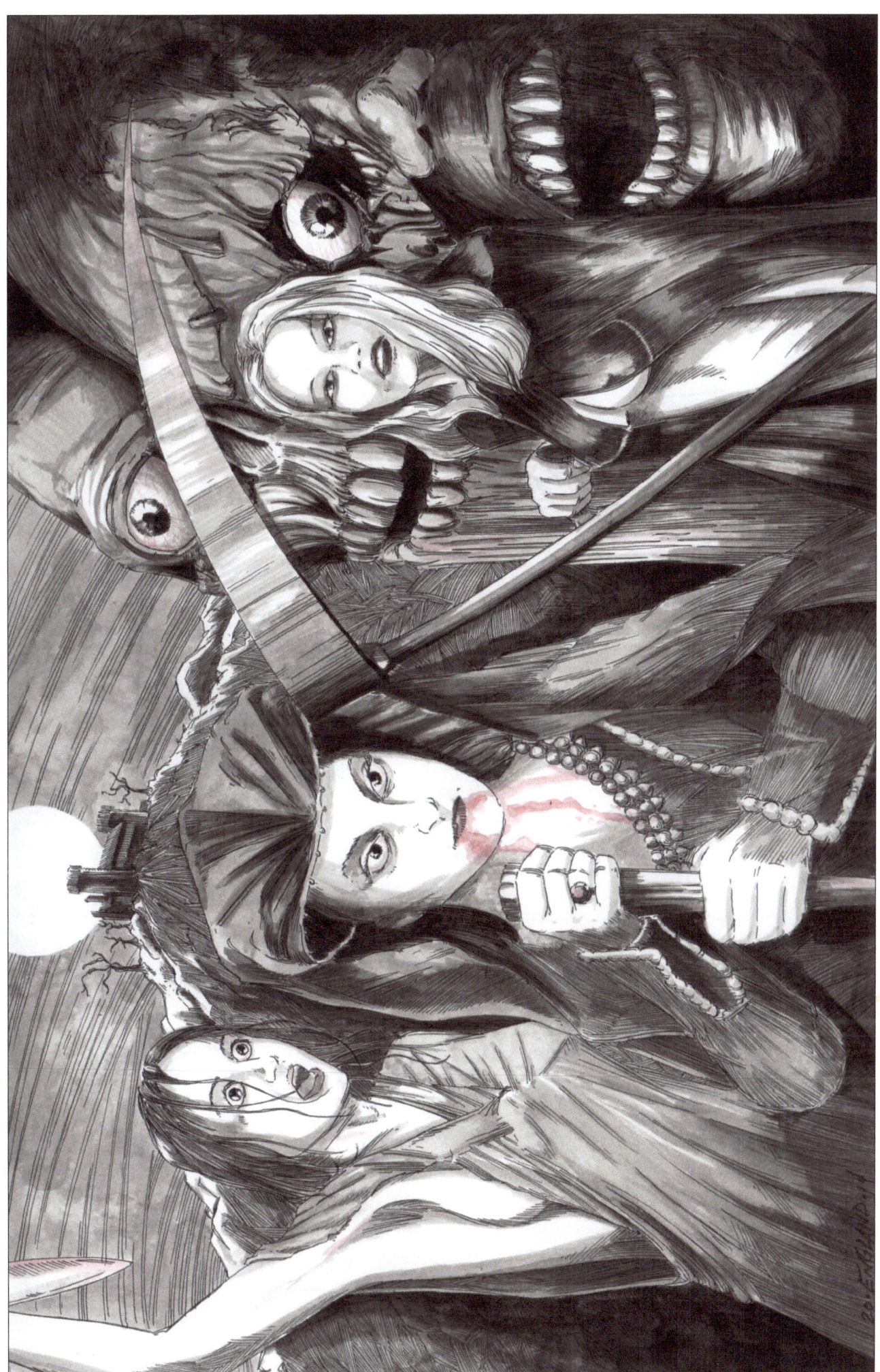

EVILSPEAK
COVER ART FOR EVILSPEAK MAGAZINE ISSUE 2
MIXED MEDIA

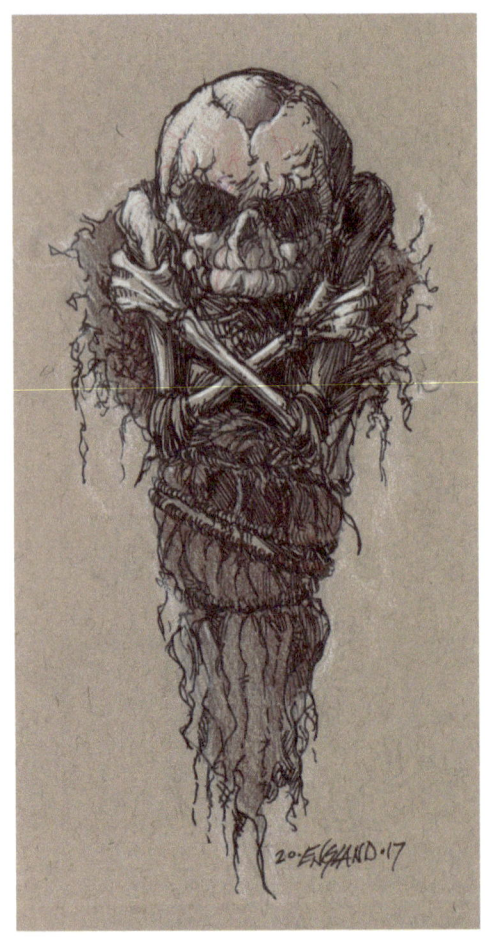
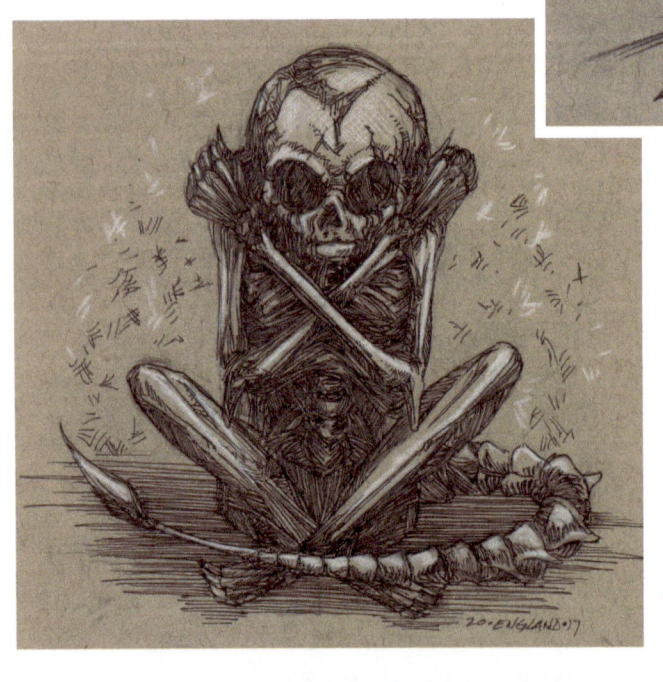

FETAL SKELETON DRAWINGS FROM 2017
INK AND PENCIL DRAWINGS

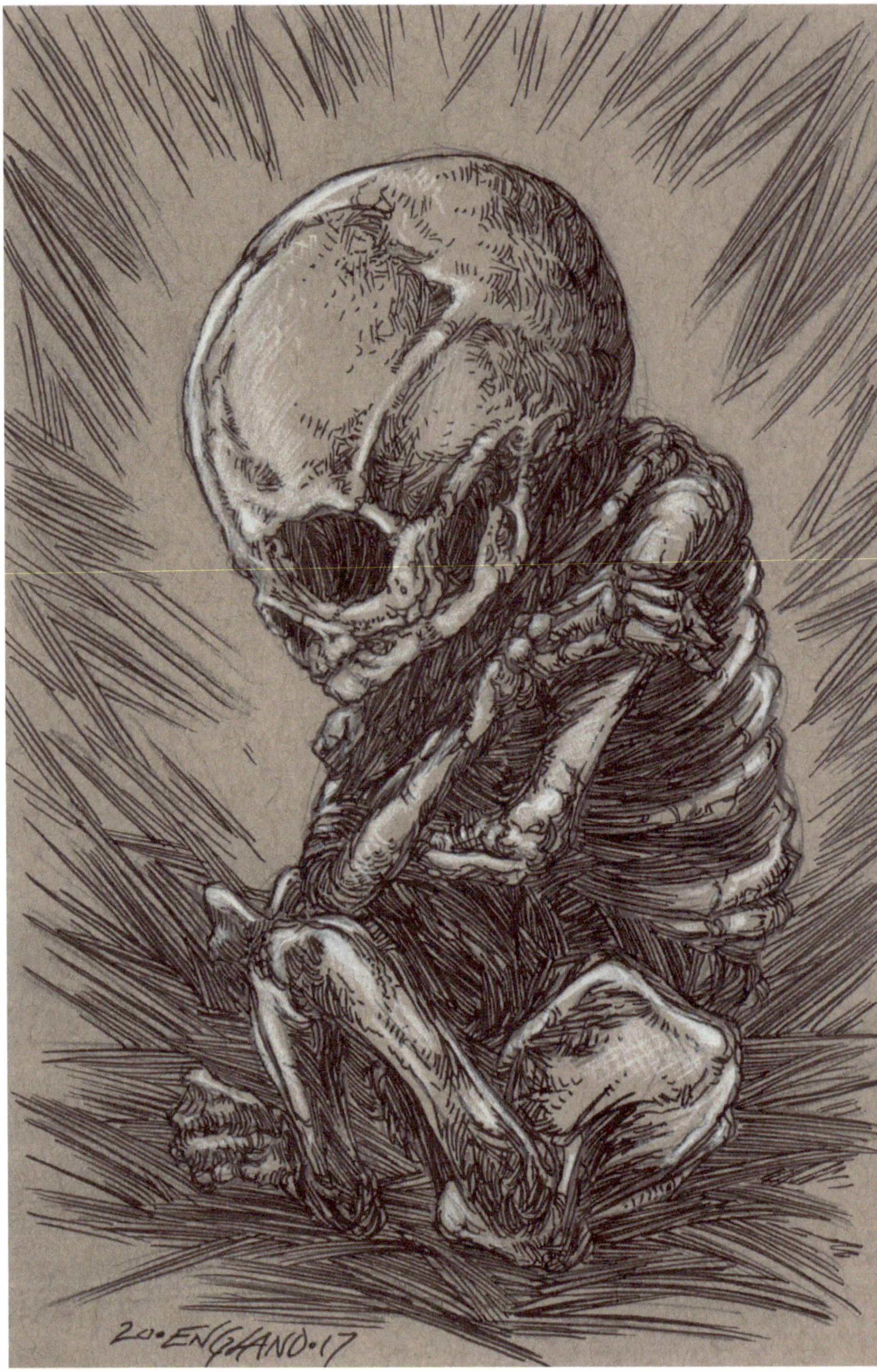

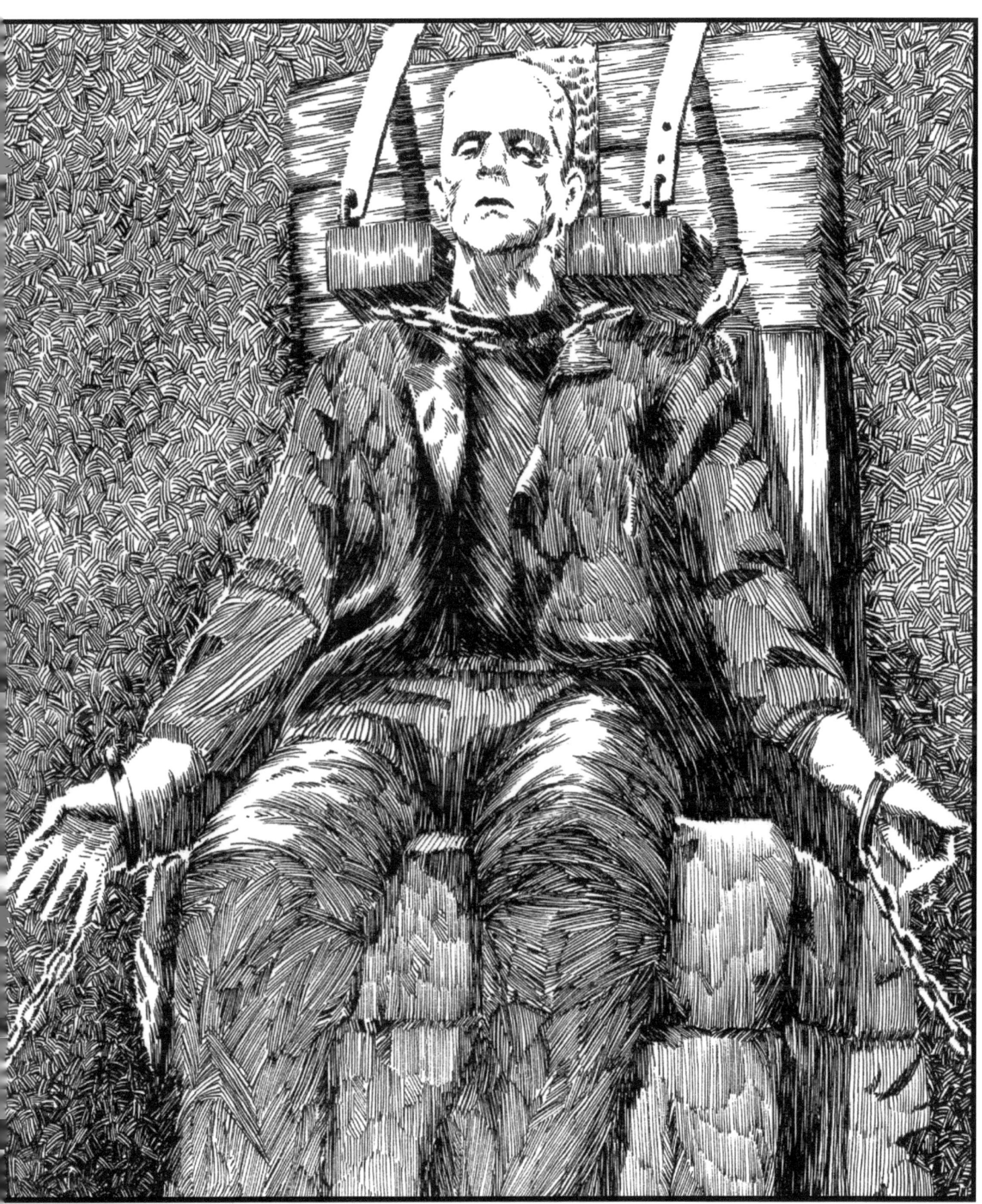

FRANKENSTEIN
PEN AND INK

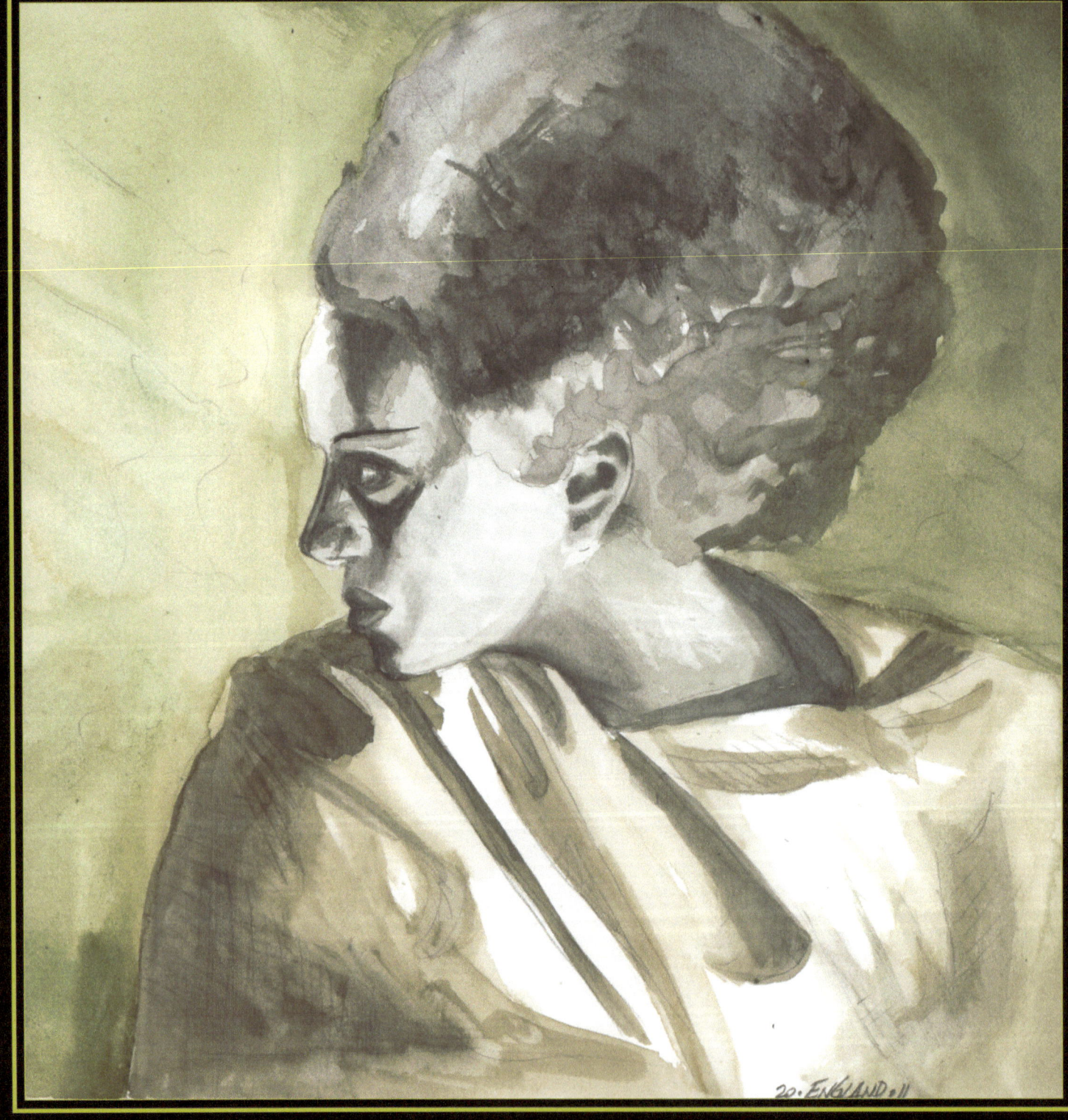

BRIDE OF FRANKENSTEIN

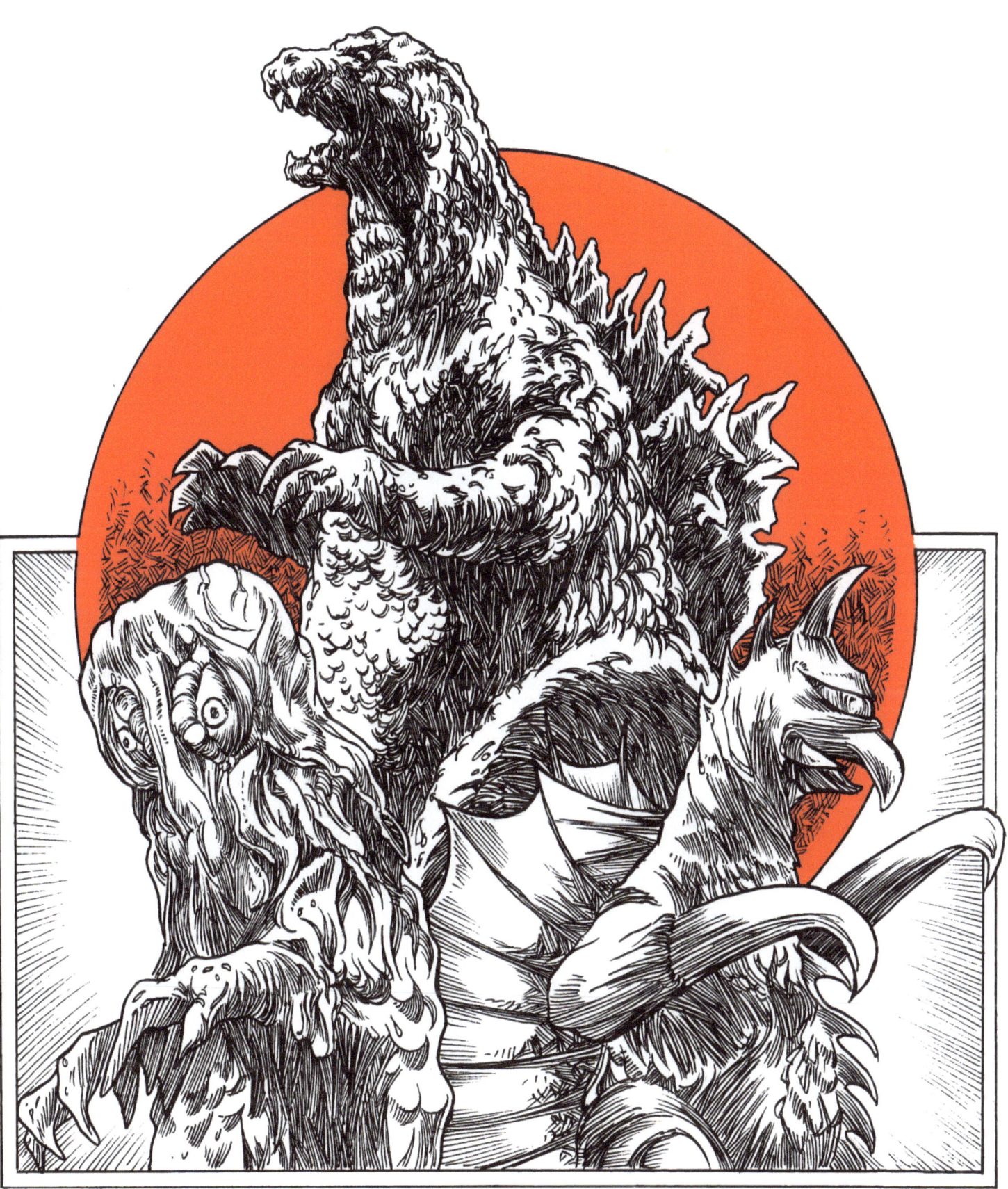

GODZILLA COMMISSION
PEN AND INK

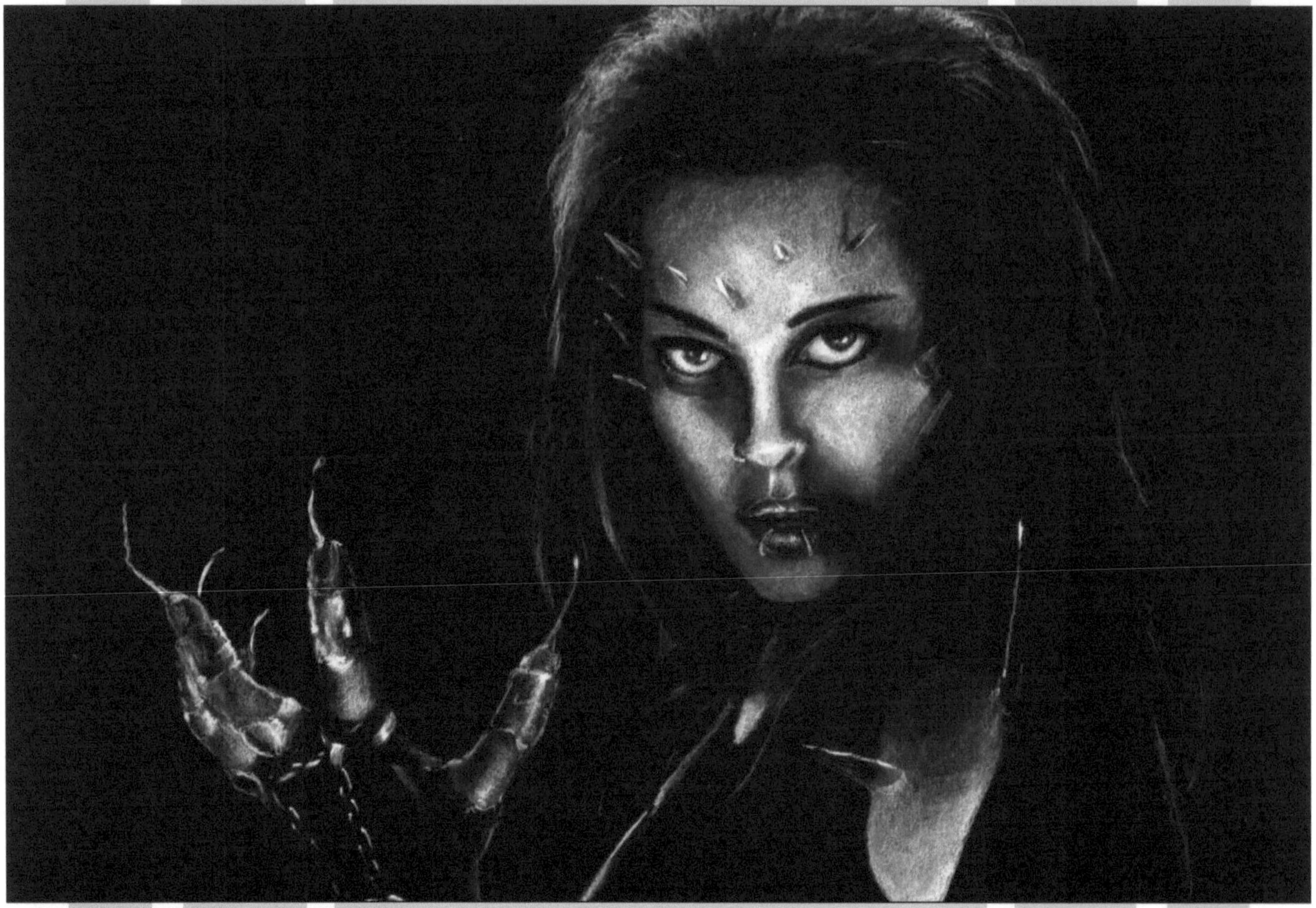

RETURN OF THE LIVING DEAD 3
WHITE CHARCOAL ON BLACK BOARD

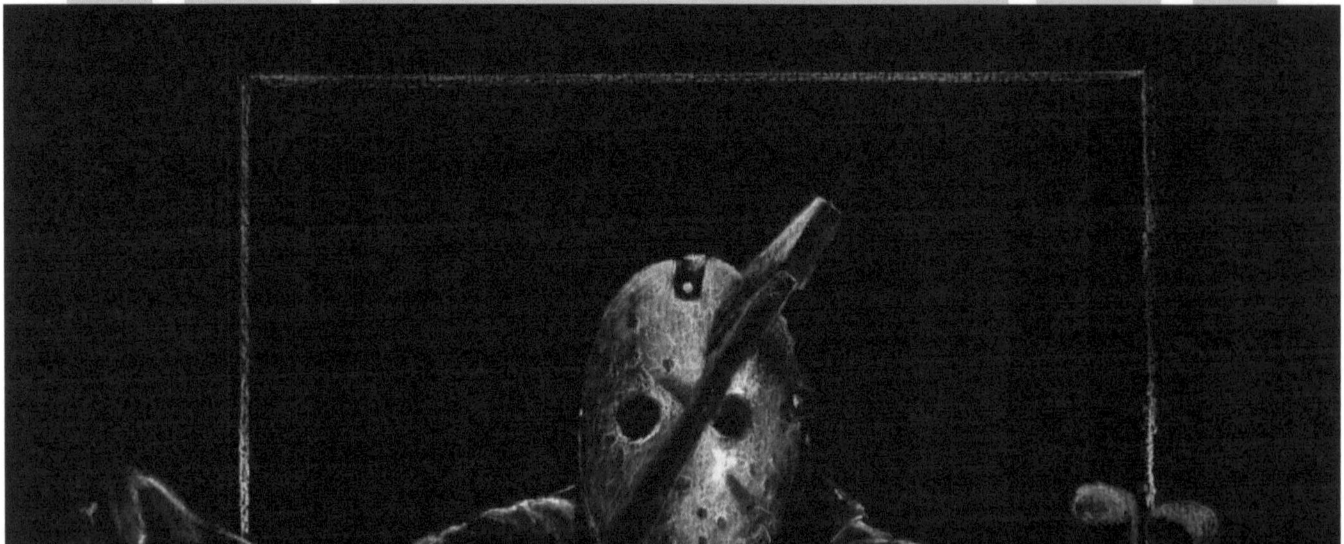

FRIDAY THE 13TH 3
WHITE CHARCOAL ON BLACK BOARD

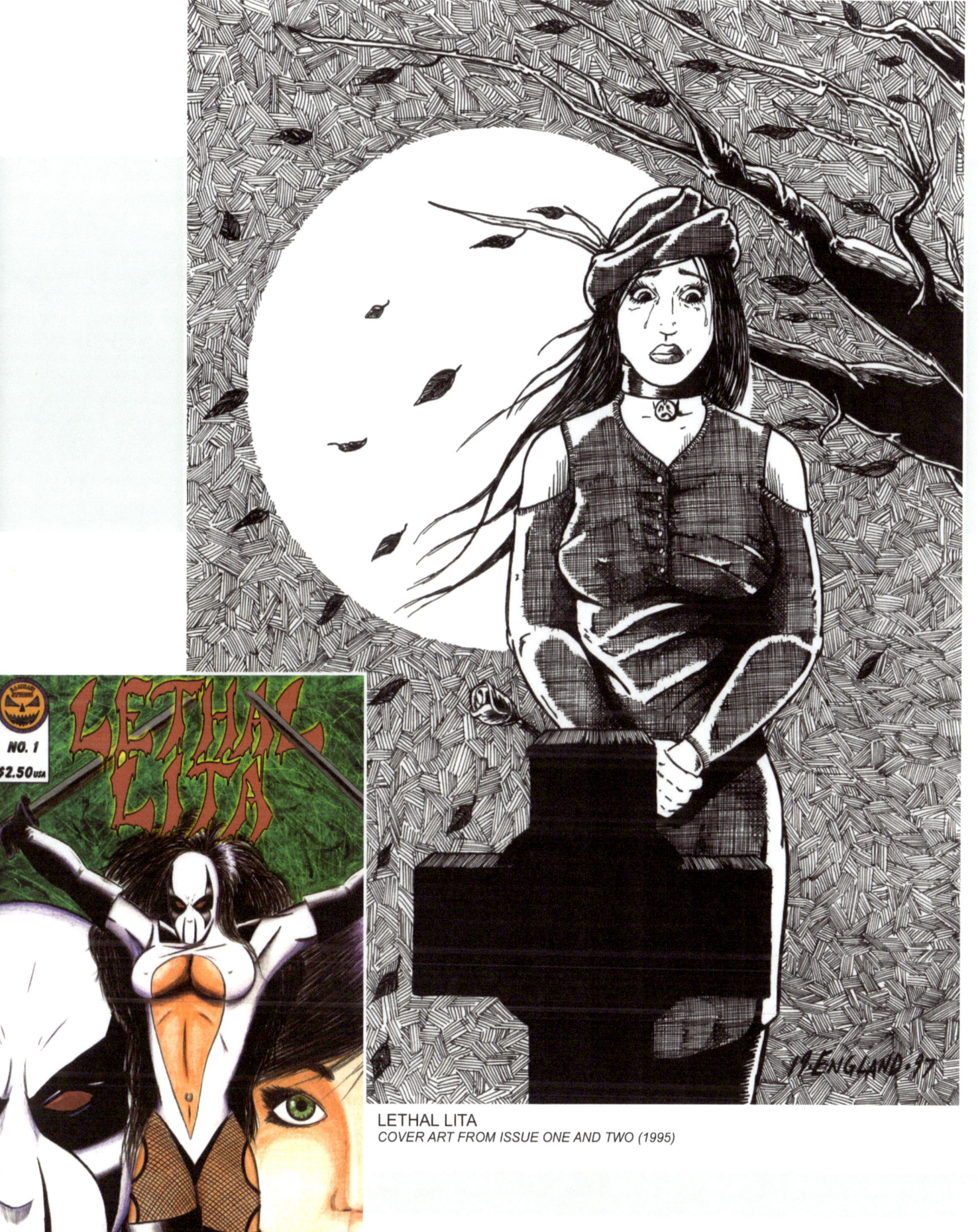

LETHAL LITA
COVER ART FROM ISSUE ONE AND TWO (1995)

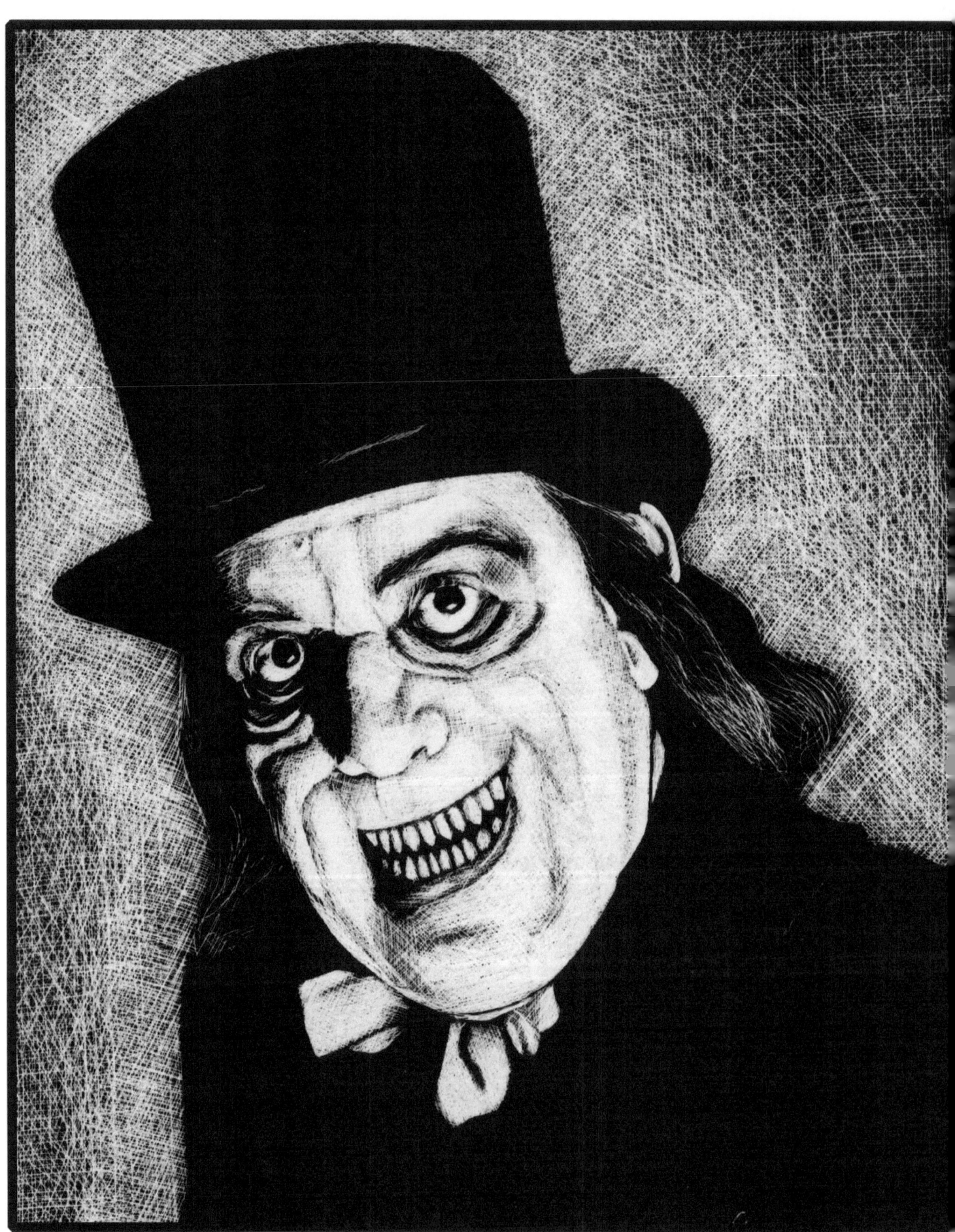

LONDON AFTER MIDNIGHT
SCRATCH BOARD

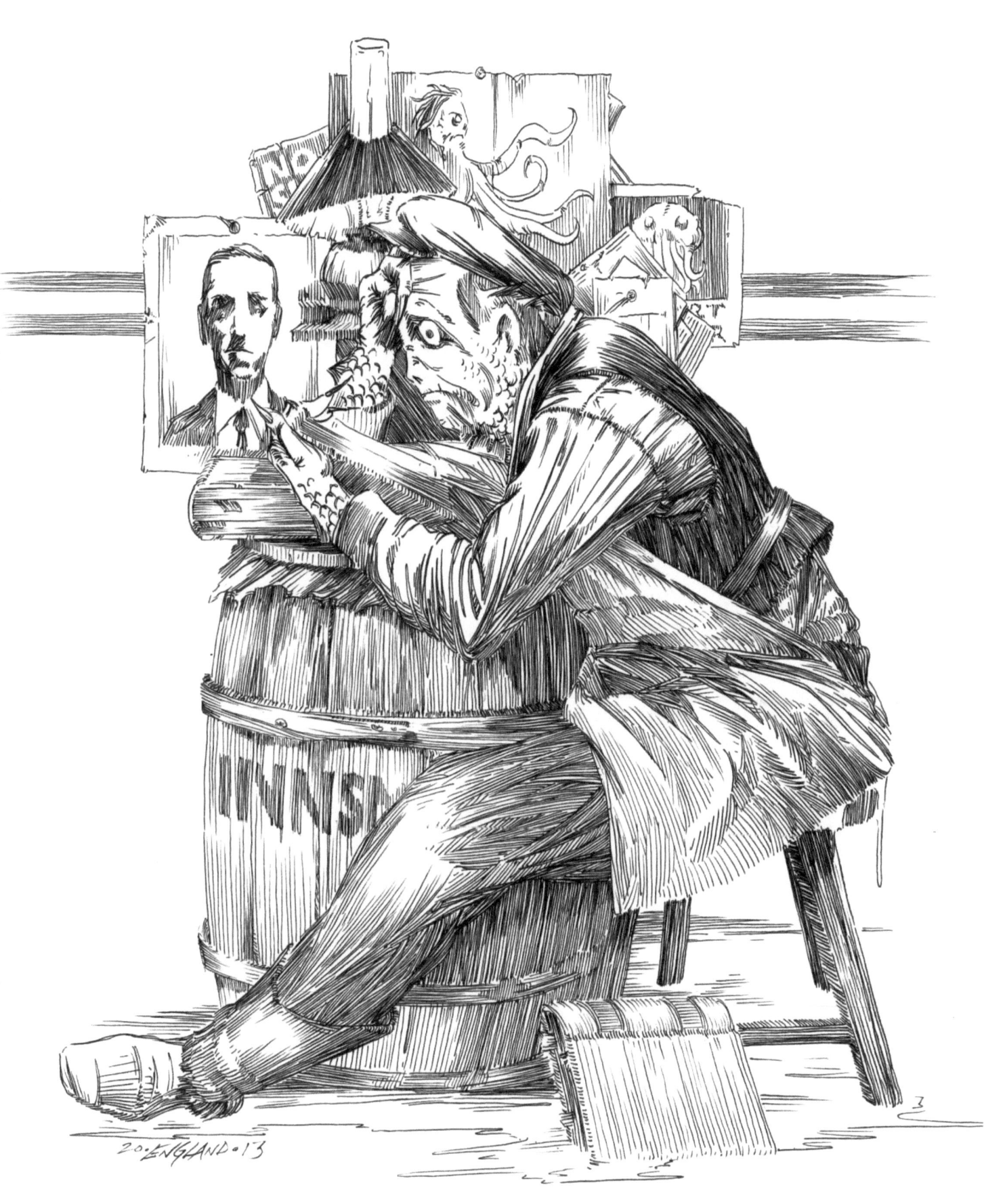

LOVECRAFT / ROCKWELL
PEN AND INK

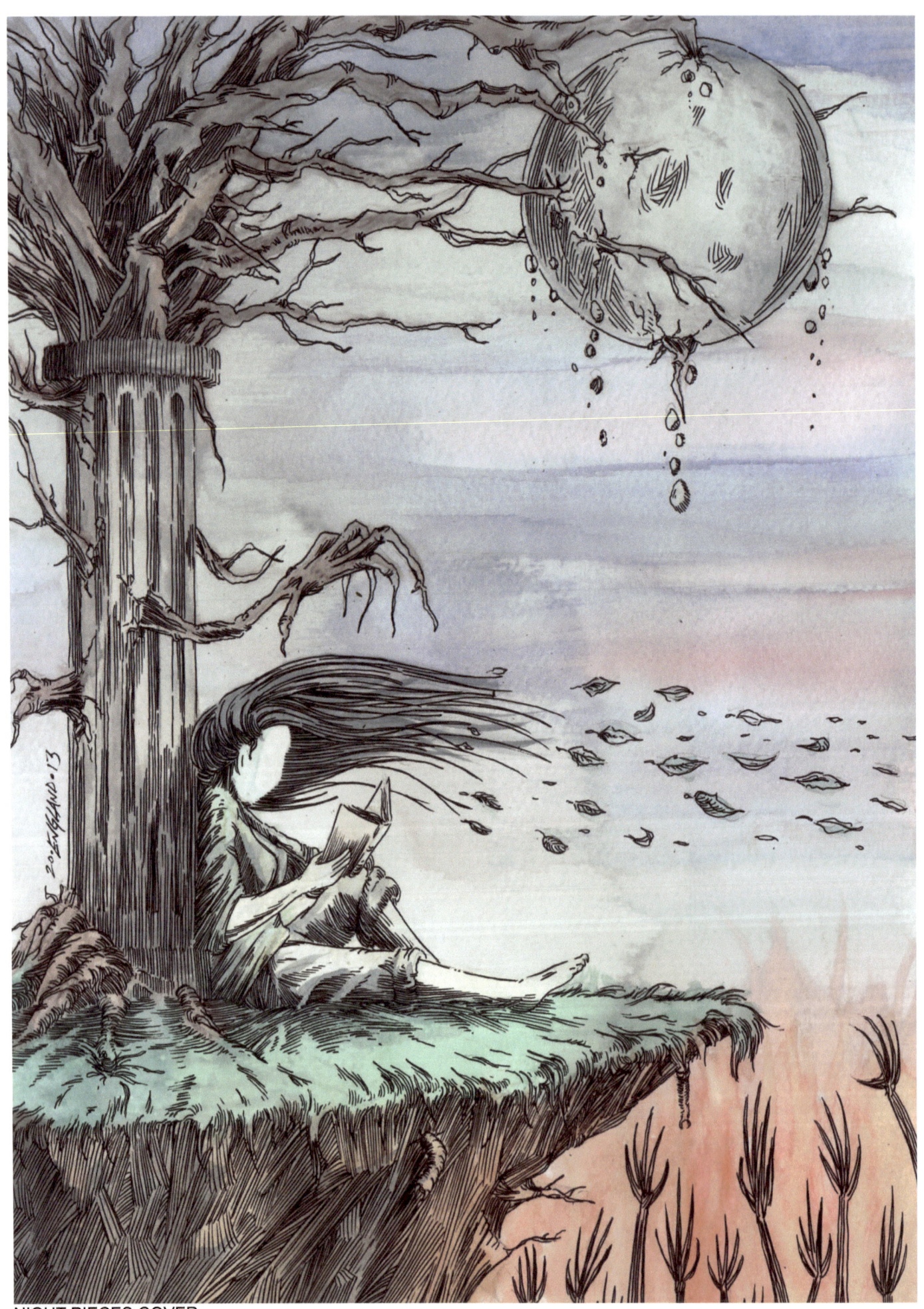

NIGHT PIECES COVER
MIXED MEDIA

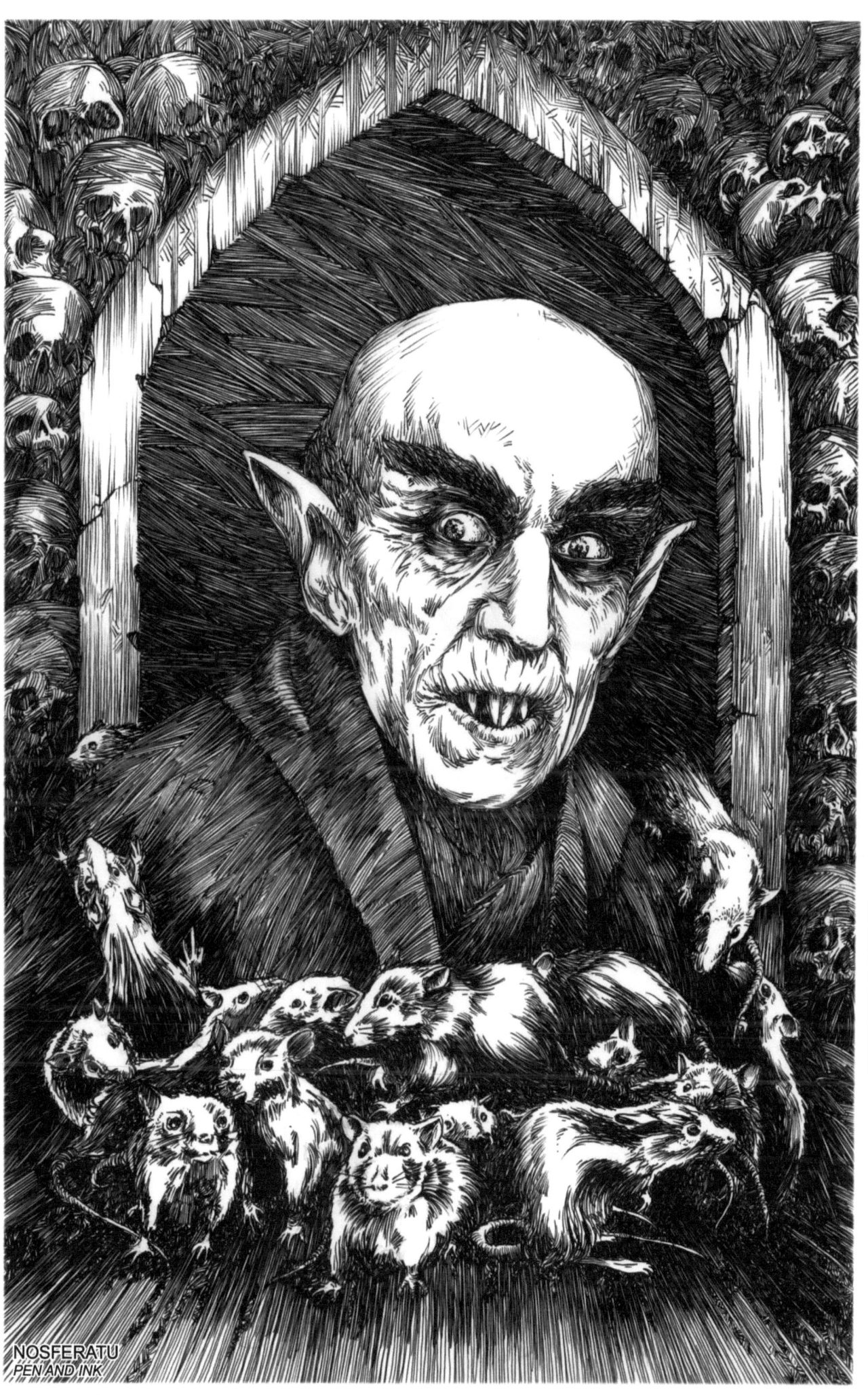

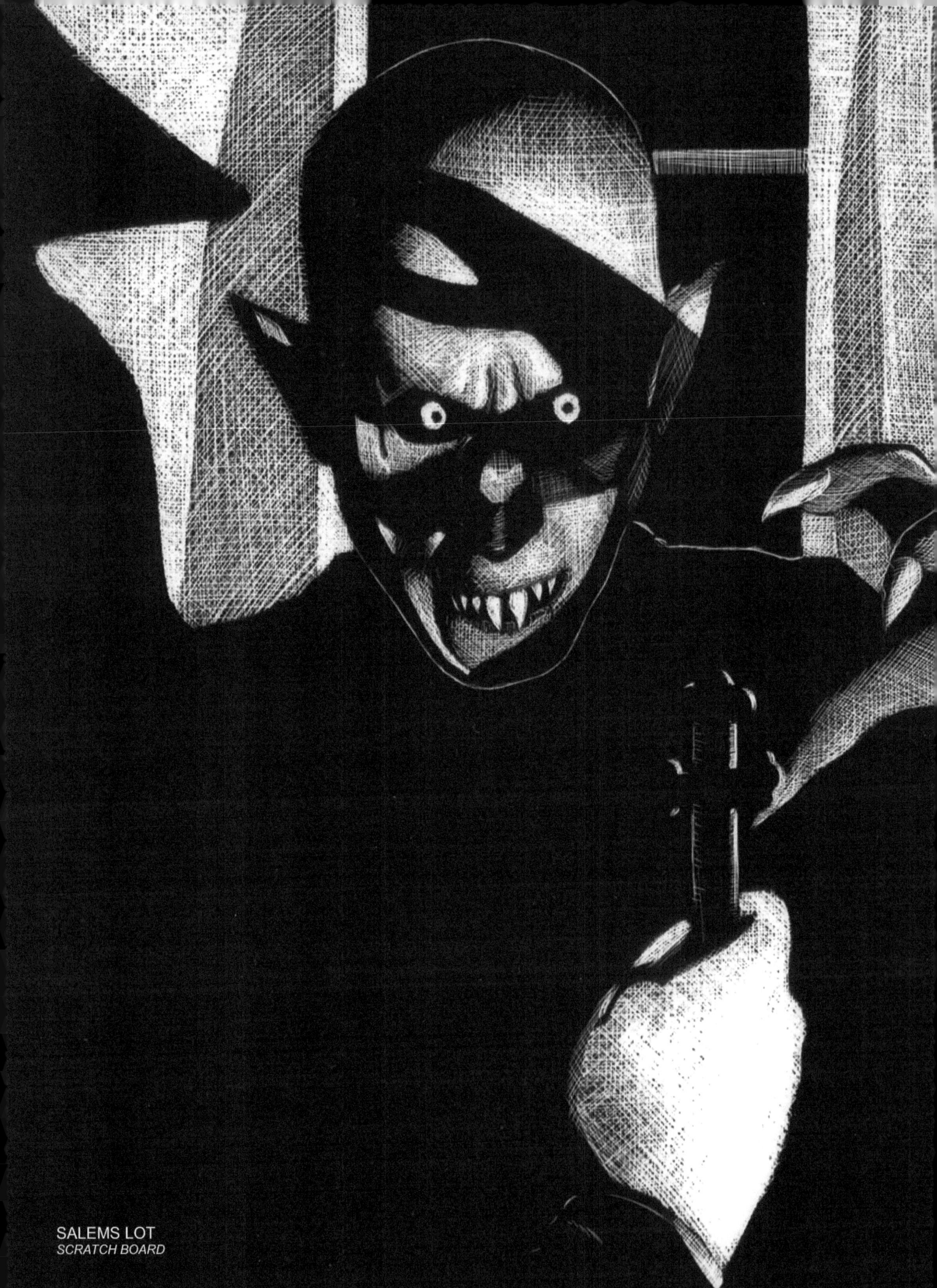

SALEM'S LOT
SCRATCH BOARD

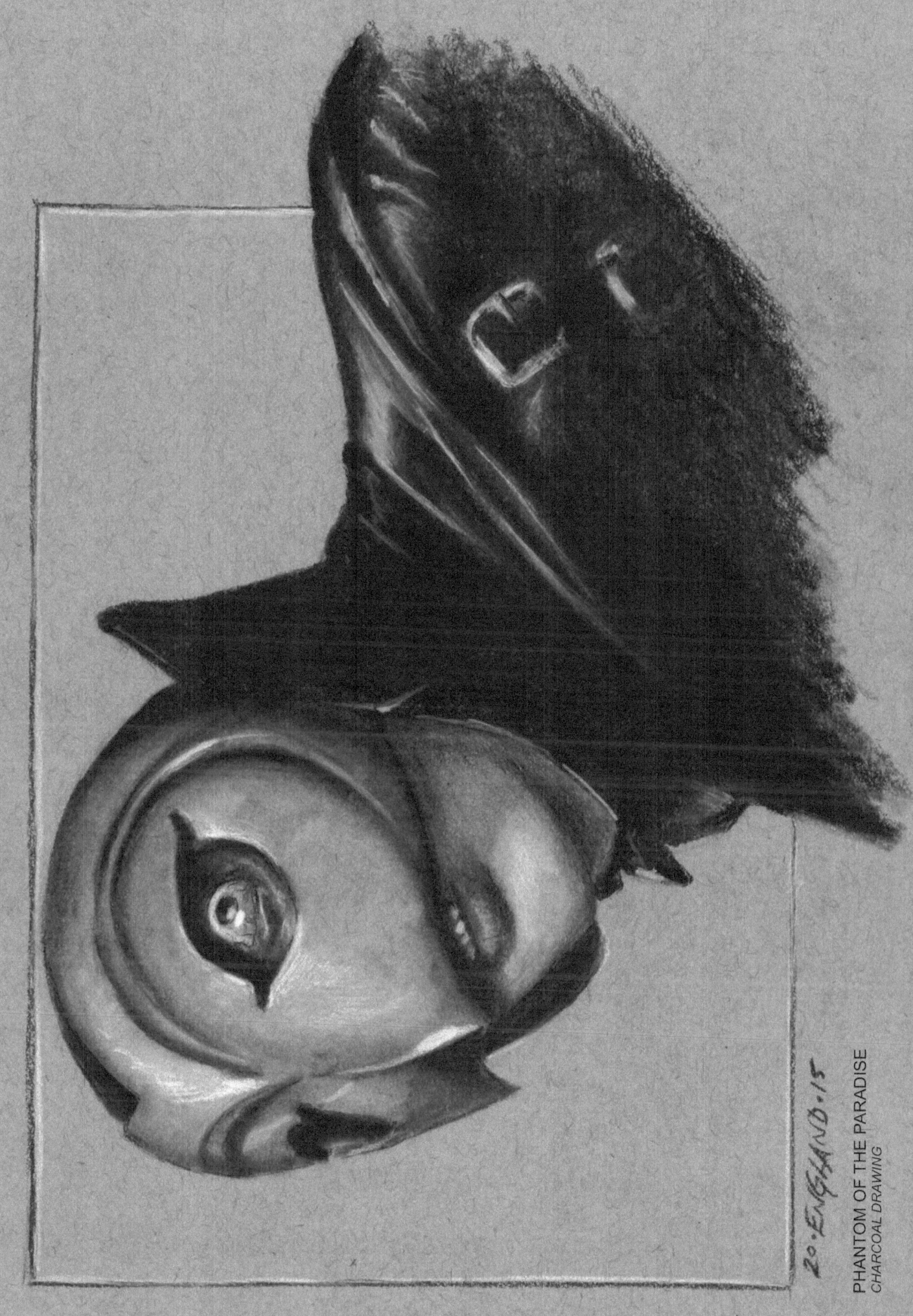

PHANTOM OF THE PARADISE
CHARCOAL DRAWING

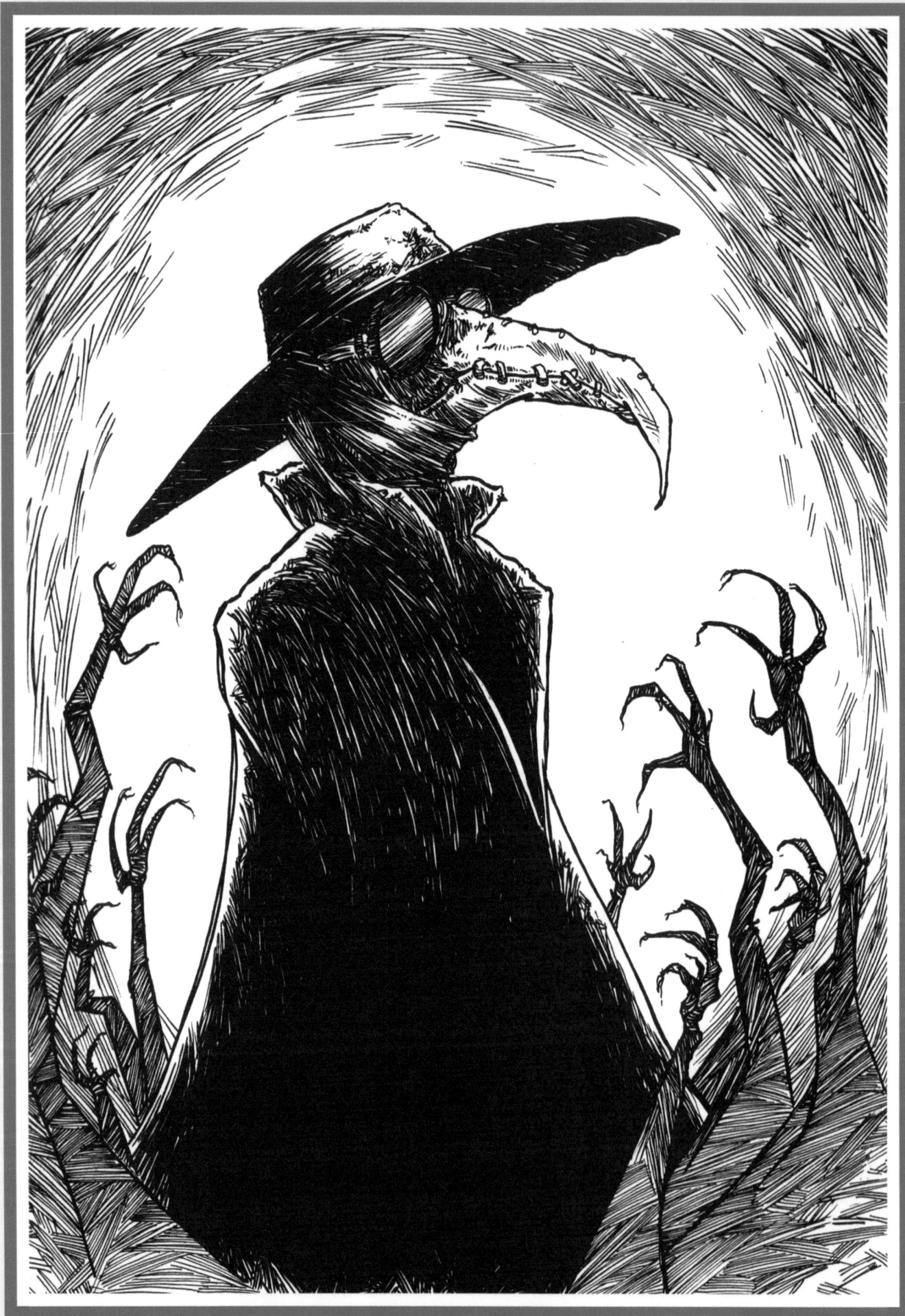

PLAGUE OF MAN
PEN AND INK

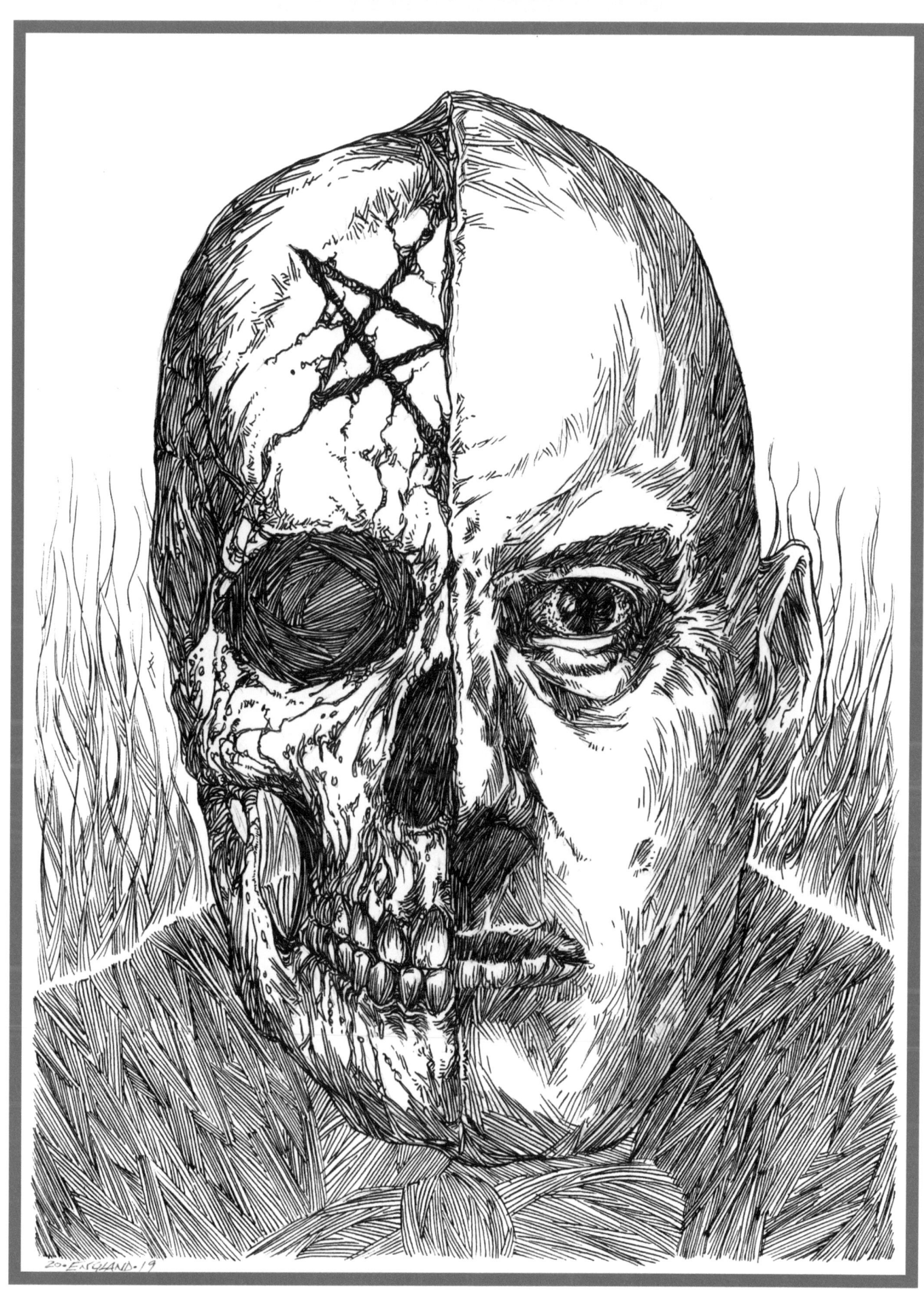

SKIN DEEP - ALEISTER CROWLEY
FOR THE HYAENA GALLERY - "DO WHAT THOU WITH" EXHIBIT

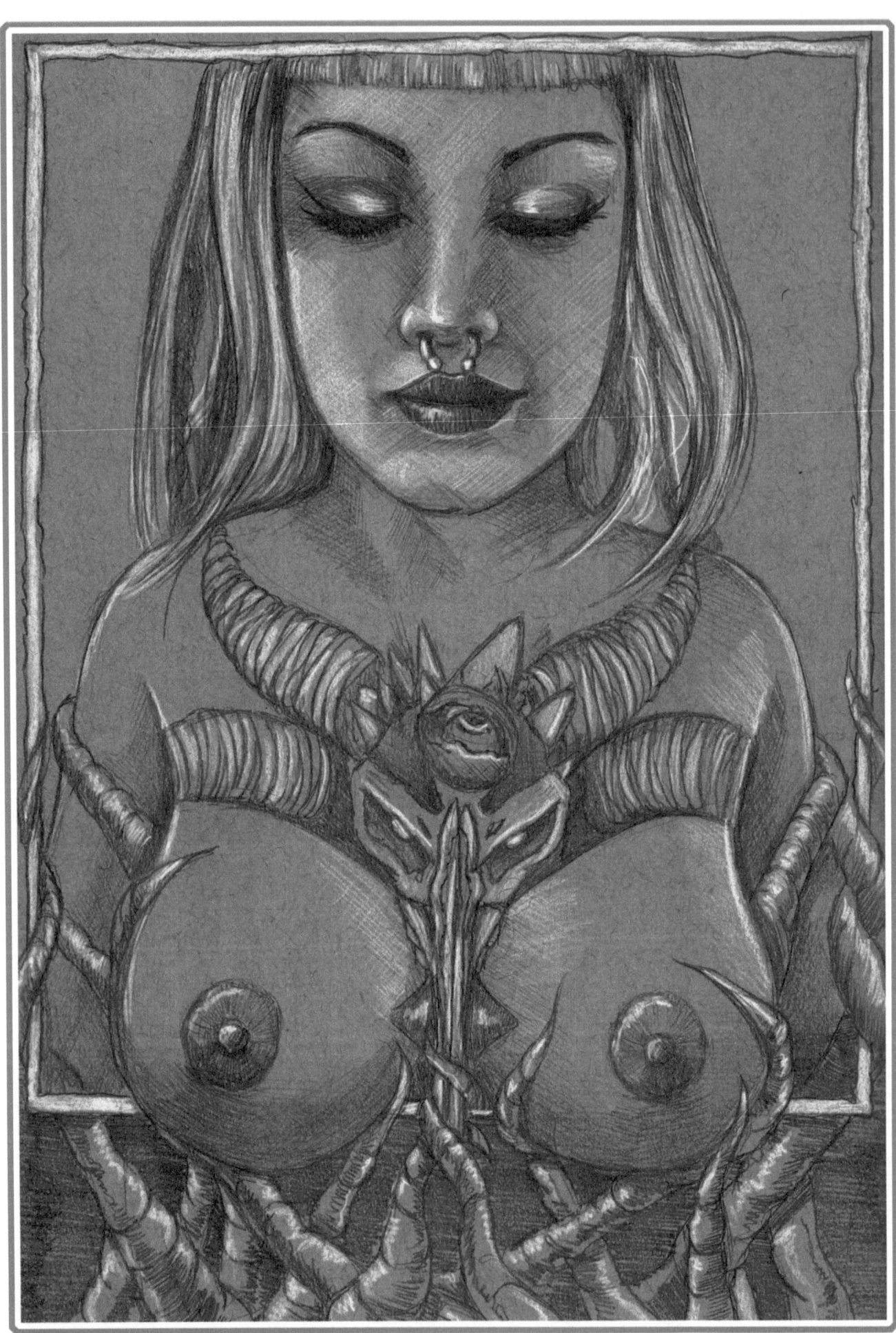

TATTOOS AND TENTACLES
PENCIL DRAWING

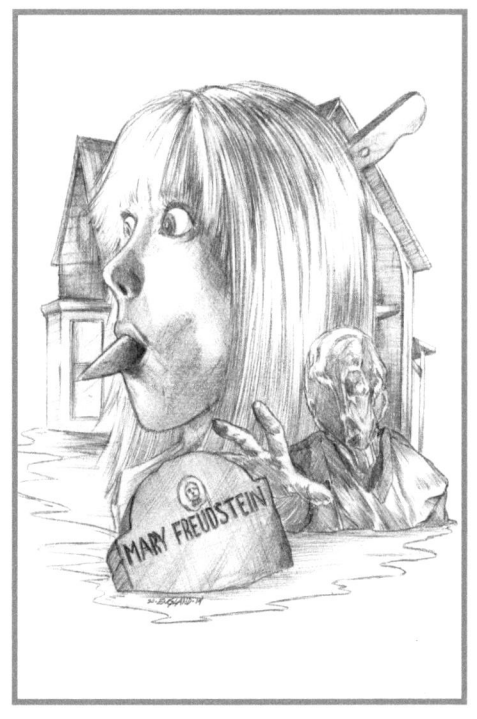
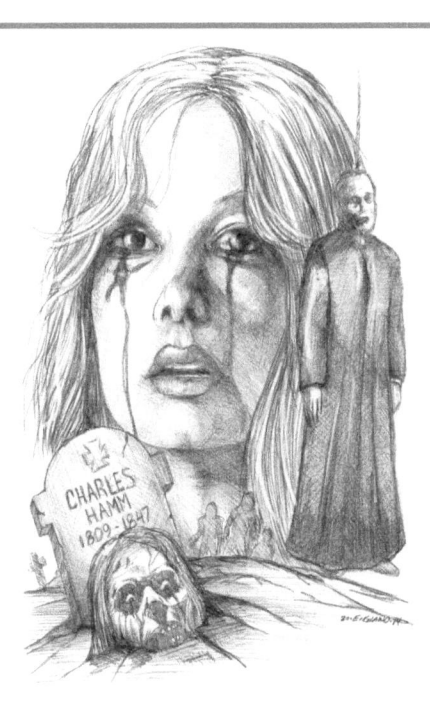
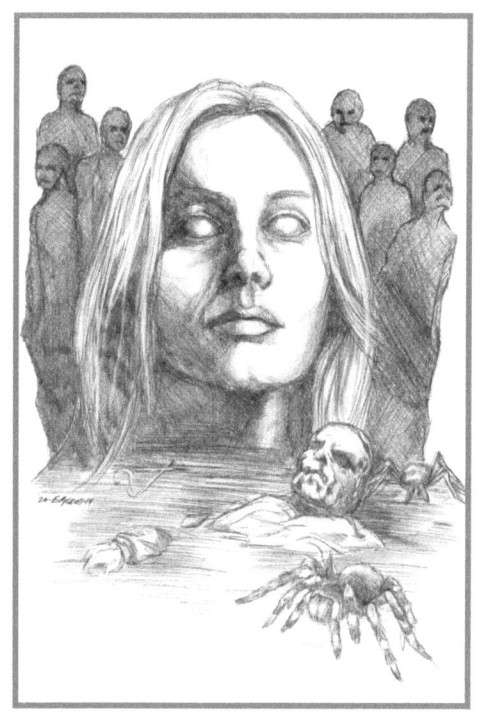

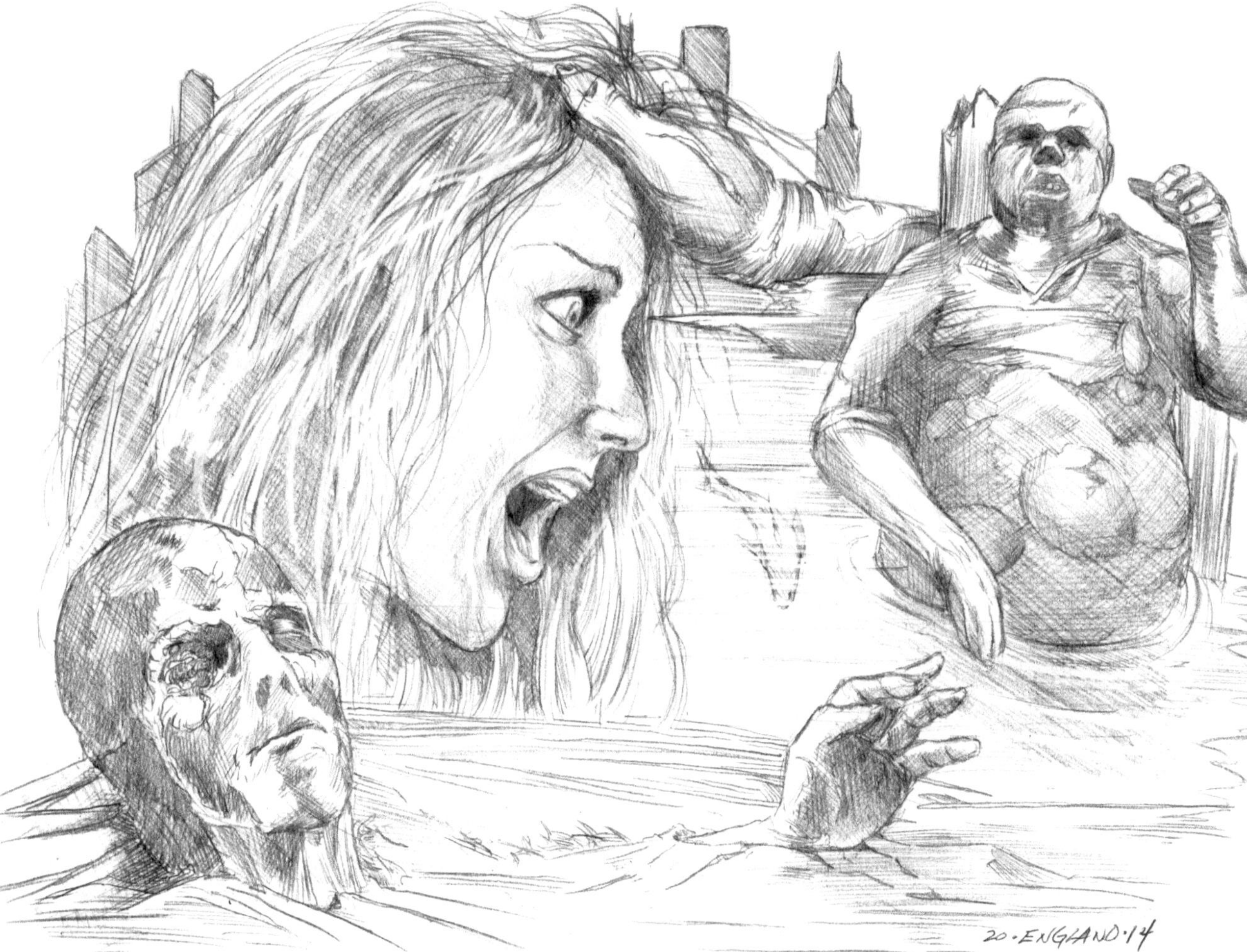

SET OF 4 LUCIO FULCI LUNCHTIME SKETCHES

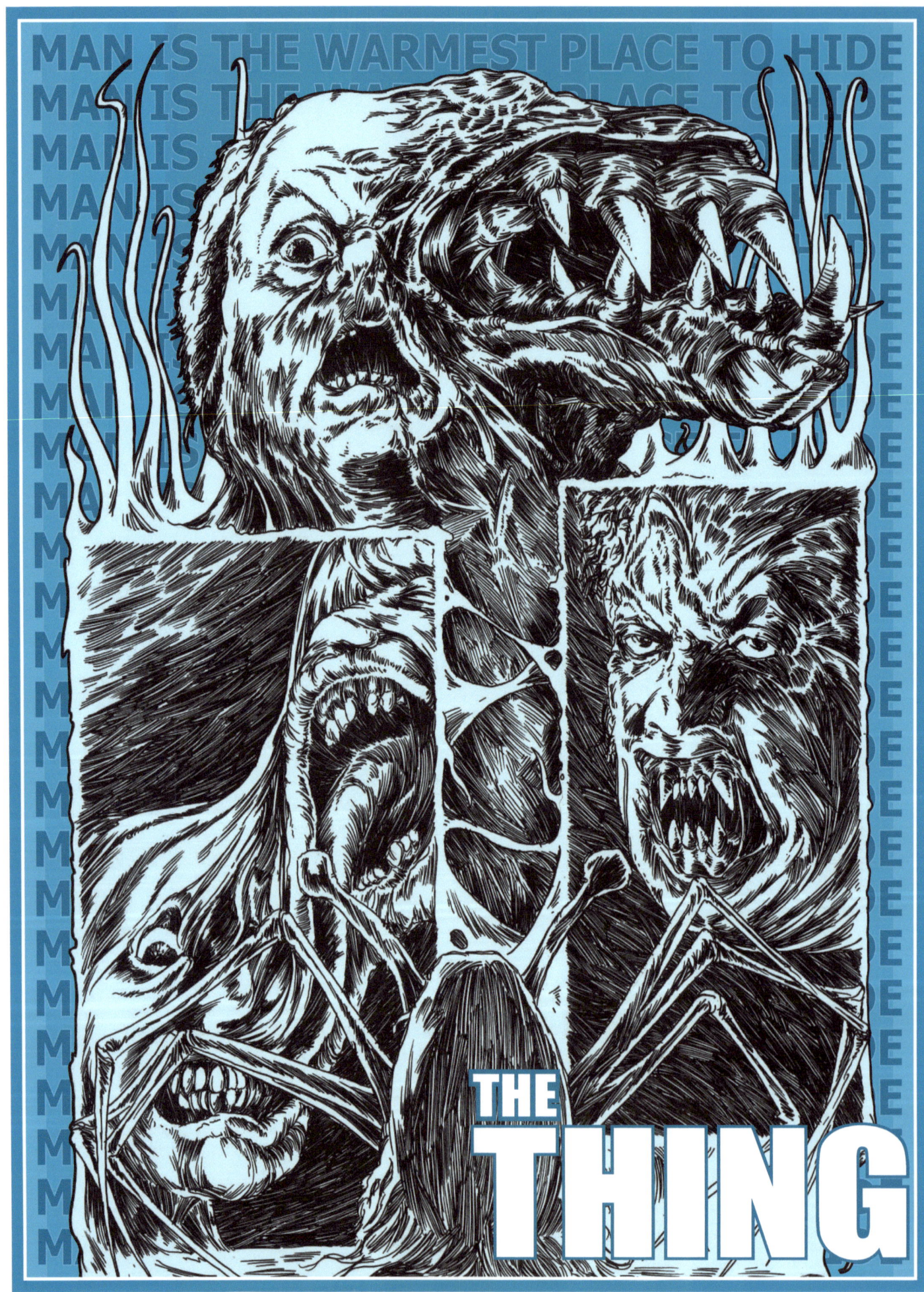

THE THING *PAGE FROM THE BOOK "THE THING ART BOOK" / MIXED MEDIA*

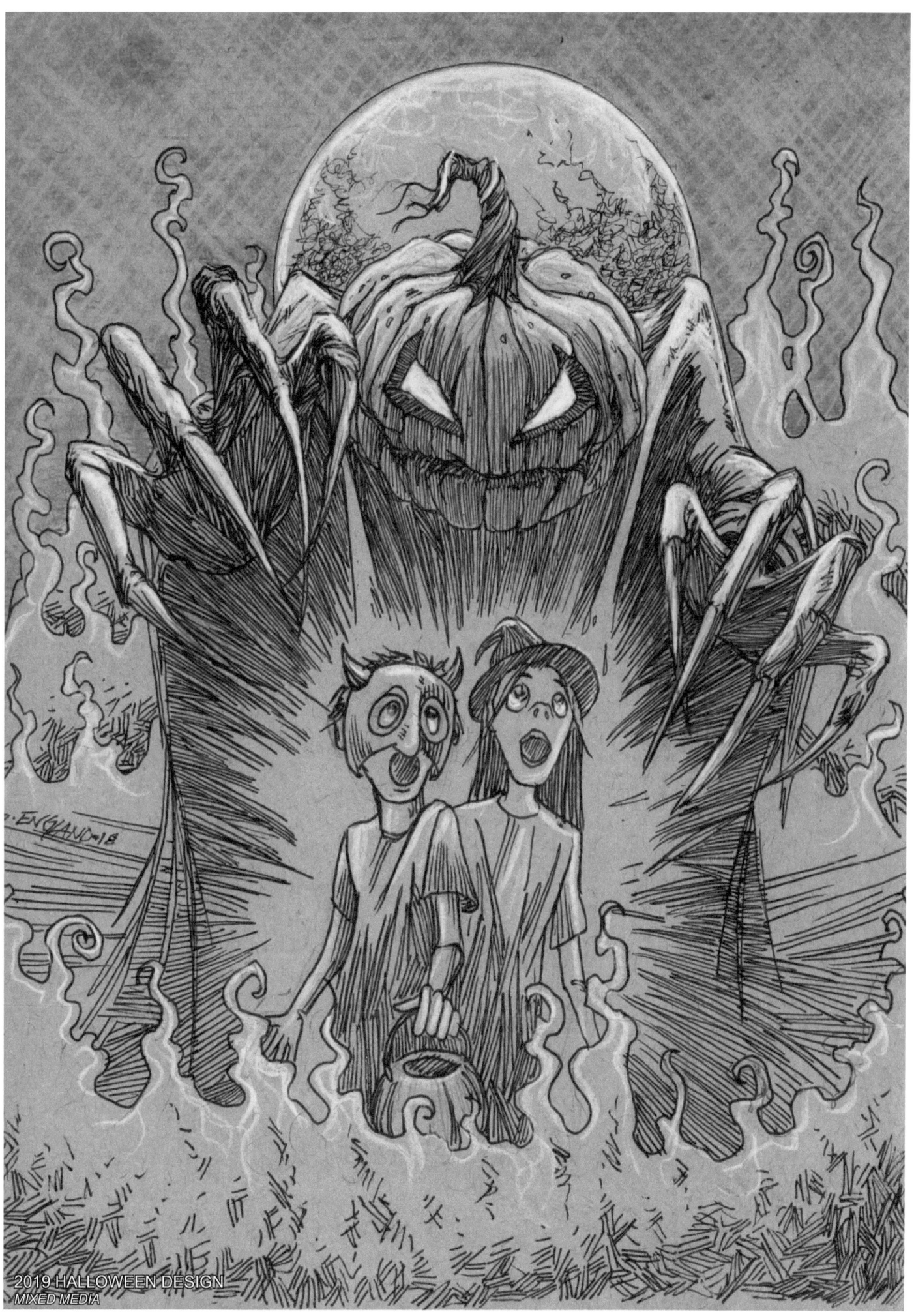

2019 HALLOWEEN DESIGN
MIXED MEDIA

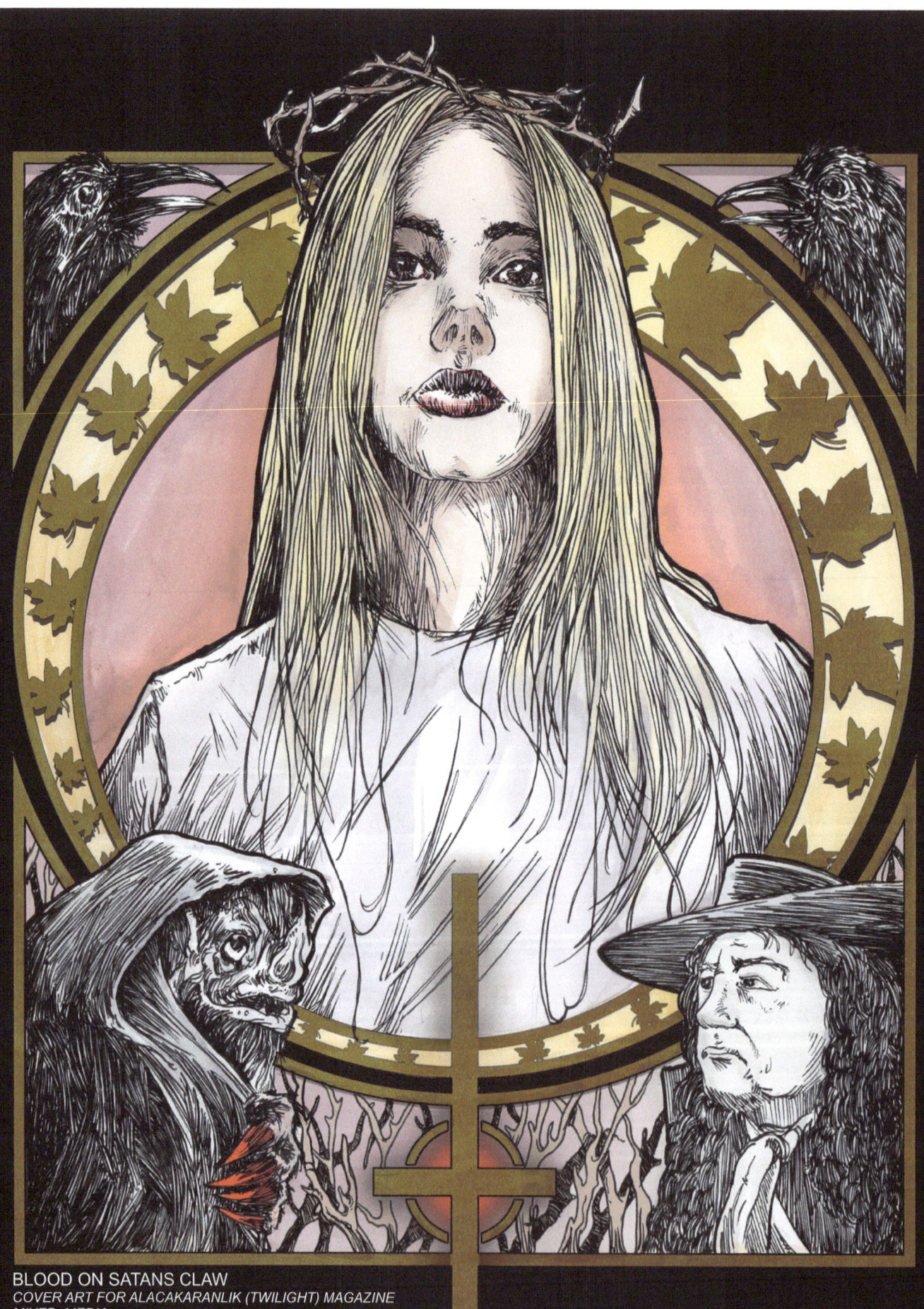

BLOOD ON SATANS CLAW
COVER ART FOR ALACAKARANLIK (TWILIGHT) MAGAZINE
MIXED MEDIA

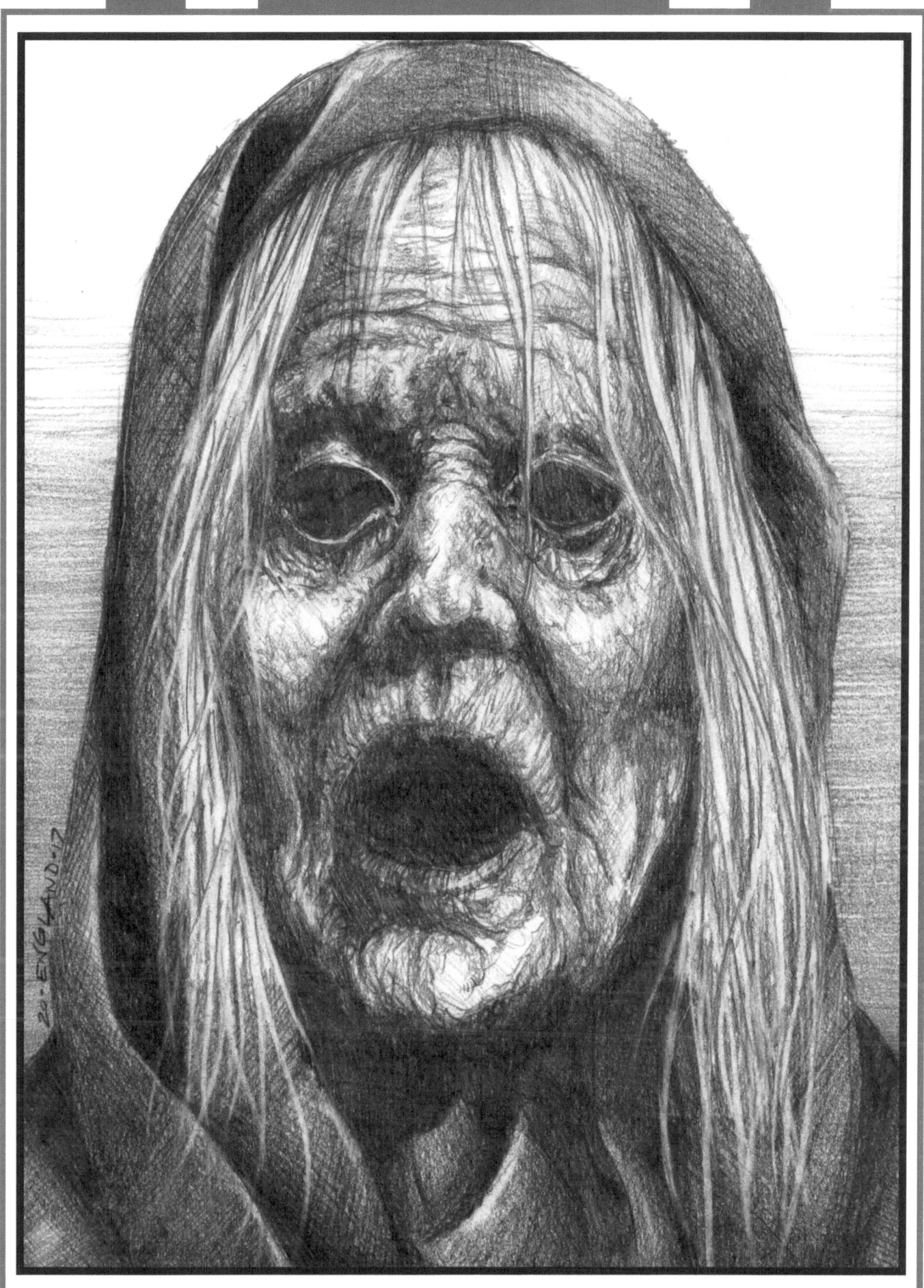

WRAITH
PENCIL DRAWING BASED ON A MASK DESIGNED BY CONNOR DELESS

All original content and characters are © Donald England 2019. All characters and titles not in the public domain remain protected pursuant to the copyright owners or claimants of the respective studios, production companies, filmmakers, authors, or other rights holders, if applicable. The inclusion herein of such characters and titles is strictly for journalistic and/or informational commentary or scholarly review and use of the same is in no way intended to imply transfer, authorization, ownership, or other claimant rights other than for such use.

www.ingramcontent.com/pod-product-compliance
Lightning Source LLC
Chambersburg PA
CBHW040455220526
45473CB00004B/1641